Colorado Cookie Collection

Written and Compiled by
CYNDI DUNCAN and GEORGIE PATRICK

C & G Publishing, Inc.
Greeley, Colorado

COLORADO COOKIE COLLECTION
DEDICATION PAGE

WE DEDICATE OUR FIRST COLORADO COOKIE
COLLECTION TO OUR CONTRIBUTORS:

Cheryl Adams	Barb Haines	Mary Ann Phillips
Joanne Andrade	Robyn Haskett	Sharon Porter
Rosie Anson	Marjean Haythorn	Kathy Pursley
Mary Aschenbrenner	Bert Hays	Mary Rae
B. J. Barrett	Carol Heinze	Lynda Reynolds
Donna Behning	Sandy Helgeson	Pam Reynolds
Pat Best	Bev Henderson	Toni Robinson
Chris Boelter	Kappy Hesse	Suzanne Roquet
Kathy Burket	Barb Howard	Sara Roy
Barb Campbell	Eileen Huff	Amy Russell
Glennda Campos	Donna Jackson	Ann Schrader
Stephanie Carlson	Paulette Jackson	Jean Schreck
Hope Cassidy	Jan Jerome	Mary Settje
Nancy Cech	Gladys Johnson	Mary Seuell
Sylvia Chinn	Gloria Johnson	Sue Simmons
Dona Cooper	Jan Kinkade	Barb Slobojan
Eileen Croissant	Judy Kinkade	Marguerite Smith
Cathy Crosier	Bobbi Kiser	Salley Smith
Sharol Darling	Becky Leonard	Gudi Spurlin
Jackie Dorn	Bonnie Lindstrom	Sheryl Steel
Bobbie Douglas	Barb Lowenbach	Nancy Steele
Sharon Dwyer	Irene Lowenbach	Pat Stoddard
Linda Etherton	Sharon Lunbeck	Betty Stookesberry
Marge Estrick	Cheryl McCluskey	Harriet Summerville
Loretta Farley	Sandy McCartey	Diane Tanner
Mary Farr	Carol Matarese	Marilyn Tapp
Pat Fay	Linda Mauch	Sandy Taubkin
Carol Feit	Linda Meeker	Pat Thomas
Zona Felderman	Ann Miller	Fern Tice
Sarah Fink	Karen Miller	Fay Ury
Suzi Fisher	Martha Minnig	Gwen Walker
Reda Foard	Becky Modlin	Brenda Webb
Carolyn Forkner	Ruth Mohrlang	Janet West
Carolyn Foster	Sharon Nickle	Leanne Windolph
Dixie Fraser	Sue Nicholas	JoLynn Winger
Kathy Freese	Hazel Oldenburg	Billie Witham
Verneine Gebbie	Libby Oliver	Hjordes Wolfe
Mary Gauthiere	Valerie Olson	Ruth Vaas
Susan Haas	Peg Osborne	Susan Young
Marge Hackett	Mary Ann Otte	

A VERY SPECIAL DEDICATION TO: Bob, Toni, Wendi, Shawn, L.G., Heidi, Wade and Heather for all of their loving patience and support!!

INTRODUCTION

The **Colorado Cookie Collection** evolved from ten years of cookie exchanges. During that time, 121 friends contributed, not only recipes, but plates of mouth-watering cookies, as well. In addition, they all arrived full of the holiday spirit and ready to have a good time.

Our first cookie exchange in 1979 got off to a rather shaky start but gave us the base on which to perfect future exchanges. The most notable problem was one of traffic congestion, the downfall of many otherwise successful gatherings. This was caused by guests lining up to copy recipes — poor planning on our part. We also found that some guests didn't realize that the purpose of the exchange was, of course, an opportunity to share the joy of the holidays with friends. The frustration that first year was compounded when we realized that when all the guests departed, there were very few cookies left for the two of us to share.

After that first year, we made some rather major changes in our approach to planning future exchanges and have devised a system that takes about 30 minutes planning time and minimal preparation, providing you host the event with a friend and share the work. Here follows what we consider to be an excellent recipe for a successful cookie exchange.

SUCCESSFUL COOKIE EXCHANGE

Note: Cyndi put her skill in calligraphy to work in invitations, name tags, place cards and the cover of the booklet.

Planning:
  1 date
  40-70 friends
  invitations

Set aside 30-60 minutes with a friend (can be held alone but isn't as much fun). Select a date. Make a list of friends, including addresses. Create your own personal invitation that can easily be changed from year to year. (Pictures from coloring books, holiday cards or your own design can be used.)

The following information should be included:
  name of the event, date, time, address, name of hosts, RSVP with cookie recipe, how many cookies to bring, how to package cookies and use a disposable container.

Preparation:
  recipe booklets
  name tags, assorted holiday shapes
  straight pins
  2 place cards per cookie
  6-10 door prizes
  bell

filled cookie jar or poinsettia
napkins
plates
coffee
tea
cups
tablecloths
decorations
pop flats
tissue paper
2-4 helpers
6 1/2 dozen cookies

Recipe booklet: Decide how you want to organize your booklet. Alphabetical, by types of cookies or by random selection (as they are received) are some alternatives. Add graphics or clip art; used greeting cards or gift wrap works great. Create a cover that easily can be adapted for next year — you don't want to recreate every year. (The Christmas tree became the symbol for our exchange. The year changed in the star on top of the tree and different cookie names were written on the decorations on the tree.) Type your recipe, make the appropriate number of copies, collate and tie with yarn. (We made the cover red or green paper and tied with red, green or white yarn.) Set aside.

Name tags: Using cookie cutters or patterns, cut holiday shapes from colored paper. Do not cut more than seven of each shape but have one for each of your guests. Write a guest's name and the name of the cookie on each shape. Pin each to a recipe booklet. Set aside.

Place cards: Make 2 per cookie, 1 for the tasting table and 1 for the exchange table. Write name of cookie and name of guest who brought it on stiff, folded paper.

Door prizes: Purchase or make 6-10 door prizes. It's best to do this right after the holidays for the following year's exchange in order to take advantage of sales. Wrap prizes. Set aside. Write name of each guest on piece of paper, fold and place in basket or bowl for drawing. Place bell with basket. Set aside.

Filled cookie jar or poinsettia: We use these for centerpieces and as the main door prize. If using cookie jar, bake an assortment of cookies and place in a decorated jar the day before the exchange. (Cookies can be baked ahead and frozen.) If using poinsettia, purchase the day before the exchange.

Supplies: Again, purchasing is best accomplished right after the holidays. We use decorated cocktail napkins and plates. (If you use solid red or green plates, it is easier to mix and match each year.) Don't forget coffee, tea, cups, tablecloths and decorations. Arrange for large coffee pot and extra tables. Collect pop flats, one per guest, for guests to use to collect cookies. Line with holiday tissue paper.

Helpers: Contact 2-4 young people to help out the day of the exchange. (We have been fortunate to have daughters to fill these positions.)

House: Clean and decorate your house. This is a good excuse to get all ready for the holidays.

Cookies: Bake your 6 1/2 dozen cookies for the exchange. If possible, bake ahead and freeze. If not, be super organized the day before the exchange to allow baking time.

Set up the day of the exchange.

Make coffee and heat water for tea. Set out cups, cream, sugar, tea and spoons. Arrange a table with booklets/name tags in alphabetical order. Place door prizes and basket in convenient location. Arrange place cards on tasting and exchange tables in alphabetical order, using guests' last names. Set plate at each place on the testing table. Give helpers instructions: take coats, take cookies to exchange table or take cookies to tasting table.

The exchange:

Greet guests at door. Helpers take coats and organize cookies. This can get hectic. Direct guests to name tags and booklets. When all guests have arrived, have helpers select cookies, one at a time, for each host. After your cookies have been gathered, ring bell, draw a name for door prize (must be present to win) and send a group to select cookies from the exchange table. Groups are sent according to the shape of their name tags and helpers monitor the gathering process. Repeat until all guests have selected cookies and all door prizes are given out. Lasts approximately 2 hours.

After each exchange, we evaluate the big event while cleaning up. Then we kick off our shoes, pour a glass of wine and share lunch with our helpers (usually fast food). Traditionally, the person not hosting the event provides the wine and brings a poinsettia to the host.

Although we still have a few bugs to work out, like training our guests to bring cookies in disposable containers, we feel that anyone can take our recipe for a successful cookie exchange and create their own holiday event.

Bar Cookies

CARAMEL LAYER CHOCOLATE SQUARES

Combine and cook over low heat until caramels are melted; stir constantly. Set aside.

  1 14-oz. package caramels
  1/3 c. evaporated milk

Grease and flour 13" × 9" pan. In large mixing bowl mix by hand until dough holds together:

  1 package German chocolate cake mix
  3/4 c. margarine, melted
  2/3 c. evaporated milk
  1 c. nuts, chopped

Press 1/2 of dough into prepared pan and bake at 350 for 6 minutes. Sprinkle 1 6-oz. package semi-sweet chocolate pieces over baked cookie crust. Spread caramel mixture over chocolate pieces. Drop reserved dough over caramel mixture in dime-sized pieces. Return to oven. Bake 15-18 minutes. Cool slightly. Refrigerate for 30 minutes to set caramel. Cut into squares.

FUDGE BARS

Blend with fork until crumbly:

  1/2 c. margarine
  1/4 c. sugar
  1 1/2 c. flour

Press into 9" × 13" pan. Bake at 325 for 20-25 minutes. Cook in double boiler over medium heat:

  1/2 c. margarine
  1/2 c. brown sugar
  1 c. sweetened condensed Eagle milk
  2 Tbsp. corn syrup

Stir constantly until it pulls away from pan. Spread over shortbread. Melt 1/2-3/4 of a 4-oz. Hershey chocolate bar and spread gently over the top.

PINEAPPLE BARS

2 1/2 c. flour
1/3 c. sugar
1/4 tsp. salt
1 egg, separated
1 c. butter, softened
1/2 c. nuts, chopped
2/3 c. pineapple, peach
   or apricot preserves

Mix well the flour, sugar and salt. Cut in butter until crumbly. Stir in egg white until well blended. Gather in ball. Cut off 1/3, wrap and chill. Press remaining dough into 9" × 13" pan. Bake in 375 oven about 12 minutes. Cool. Spread with thin layer preserves. Sprinkle with nuts. Roll out chilled dough 1/8" thick; cut 1/2" strips with pastry wheel and criss-cross over preserves. Leave 3/4" between strips. Brush strips with slightly beaten egg yolk. Bake in preheated 375 oven until golden brown, 15 minutes. Cool before cutting. Store in airtight container in cool, dry place. Makes about 32.

🌲 🌲 🌲 🌲 🌲

LIME BARS

Mix together:
   2 c. flour
   1 c. butter
   1/2 c. powdered sugar
Press into 13" × 9" pan. Bake at 350 for 20-25 minutes.
Beat: 4 eggs.
Add: 2 c. sugar
      Dash of salt
Add: 1/3 c. lime juice
      Few drops green food color
Beat together.
Pour over hot crust.
Bake at 350 for 20-25 minutes or until golden.
Sprinkle with powdered sugar. Cool.
Cut into bars.

PRALINE SQUARES

1 3/4 c. lightly salted butter or margarine, at room temperature
1 1/2 c. light brown sugar, packed to measure
1/4 c. granulated sugar
1/2 tsp. salt
Yolk of 1 large egg
1 c. pecans or walnuts, chopped
1 tsp. vanilla
2 c. all-purpose flour

Heat oven to 350. In a medium-sized bowl, beat butter (1 cup), 3/4 cup of the brown sugar and the granulated sugar. When creamy, beat in egg yolk, vanilla and salt. Stir in 1/2 c. of the nuts and then the flour. Press dough evenly into a 15" × 10" × 1" baking pan. Bake 15 minutes. Meanwhile, combine remaining 3/4 c. butter and brown sugar in a small saucepan. Bring to a boil over high heat and boil 3 minutes, stirring constantly. Remove baking pan from oven and prick dough all over with a fork. Pour sugar syrup over dough and spread evenly. Return to oven and bake 5 minutes longer. Remove from oven and place on wire rack; immediately sprinkle with remaining 1/2 c. nuts. Cool 15 minutes and cut into 1" squares. Let cool completely before removing from pan.

LEMON CHEESE BARS

1 yellow cake mix
2 eggs
1 stick margarine, melted
1 Tbsp. lemon juice

Mix to pie dough consistency and press into bottom of a jelly roll pan or cookie sheet with sides.

Filling:
1 8-oz. package cream cheese
2 eggs
1 2/3 c. powdered sugar

Blend cream cheese and eggs. Add powedered sugar.

Pour over dough and bake at 350 for approximately 20 minutes. Watch the top - not too brown. Makes 3 1/2 dozen.

NANCY REAGAN'S FAVORITE COOKIES

1 c. margarine at room temperature
3/4 c. sugar
1/4 tsp. salt
2 large egg yolks
2 1/2 c. flour
1/2 c. red currant or red raspberry preserves
4 large egg whites
3/4 c. sugar
2 c. walnuts, finely chopped

In large bowl, combine margarine and 3/4 c. sugar. Beat in salt and egg yolks. Gradually add flour. Knead until smooth. Spread into greased 17" × 12" jelly roll pan. Bake 15 minutes at 350. Cool and spread evenly with preserves.

Beat egg whites until foamy. Gradually add 3/4 c. sugar and beat until stiff peaks. Blend in nuts. Spread over preserves, covering completely. Bake 25 minutes at 350. Cool 15 minutes and cut into bars.

🌲 🌲 🌲 🌲 🌲

CHOCOLATE MINT STICKS

Melt in double boiler:
    2 squares chocolate
    1/2 c. butter
Beat together:
    2 eggs
    1 c. sugar
Add:
    1/2 c. flour
    1/4 tsp. salt
    1/4 tsp. peppermint
Add:
    1/2 c. nuts
    chocolate mixture
Bake in greased 9" × 9" pan for 20-25 minutes. Cool.

Filling:
    1 c. powdered sugar
    2 Tbsp. soft butter
    1 Tbsp. cream
    3/4 tsp. peppermint
Beat. Spread thin layer over cake. Chill until firm.
Glaze:
    1 square chocolate
    1 Tbsp. butter
Melt together in double boiler or microwave and spread over filling. Cool. Keep refrigerated.

BUTTERSCOTCH BARS

1/2 c. butter or margarine
2 c. brown sugar
2 eggs
1 tsp. vanilla
2 c. flour
2 tsp. baking powder
1/4 tsp. salt
1 c. shredded coconut
1 c. walnuts, chopped

In saucepan combine butter and brown sugar. Cook over low heat until bubbly, stirring constantly. Cool. Add eggs to mixture, one at a time, beating well after each. Add vanilla. Sift together dry ingredients; add with coconut and nuts to brown sugar mixture; mix thoroughly. Spread in greased 15 1/2" × 10 1/2" × 1" jelly roll pan. Bake in 350 oven about 25 minutes. Cut into bars while warm. Remove from pan when almost cool. Makes 3 dozen.

PUMPKIN BARS

Delicious, easy and ingredients usually on hand.

Mix:
4 eggs
2 c. pumpkin
1 c. oil
2 c. sugar
2 c. flour
2 tsp. cinnamon
1/2 tsp. salt
1 tsp. soda

Cover jelly roll pan with foil. Spread batter. Bake at 350 for 20 minutes. Add 1/2 c. nuts and/or raisins, if desired. Frost.

Icing:
3 oz. cream cheese
1 tsp. vanilla
3/4 stick margarine
2 Tbsp. milk
1 2/3 c. powdered sugar

Beat together and spread over bars.

CANDY BAR COOKIES

Cream:
   3/4 c. butter
   3/4 c. sifted brown sugar
Add and mix well:
   1 tsp. vanilla
   2 Tbsp. evaporated milk
   1/4 tsp. salt
Blend in:
   2-2 1/2 c. flour (make dough easy to roll and transfer to cookie sheet)
Roll out dough, 1/2 at a time, to 12" × 18" rectangle. Cut into 2" squares. Bake at 325 for 12-16 minutes, until lightly brown. Cool.

Caramel Filling:
   Melt 28 light caramels and 1/4 c. evaporated milk in top of double boiler or microwave. Remove from heat and stir in 1/4 c. butter, 1 c. sifted powdered sugar and 1 c. chopped pecans. Top each cookie with 1 tsp. of this filling.

Chocolate Icing:
   Melt 1 c. milk chocolate chips in pan with 1/3 c. evaporated milk. (Can use microwave). Remove from heat and stir in 2 Tbsp. butter, 1 tsp. vanilla and 1/2 c. sifted powdered sugar. Top each cookie with 1/2 tsp. of this and a pecan half.

Makes 4 dozen cookies.

🌲   🌲   🌲   🌲   🌲

RASPBERRY BARS

   3/4 c. margarine
   1 c. brown sugar, packed
   1 1/2 c. flour
   1 tsp. salt
   1/2 tsp. soda
   1 1/2 c. oatmeal
   10 oz. raspberry jam
Cream margarine and sugar until fluffy. Add dry ingredients, mix well. Press 1/2 of mixture into greased 9" × 13" pan. Spread with jam. Press rest of crumbs on top. Bake at 400 for 20-25 minutes.

6

HOLLY SQUARES

1 c. flour
1 tsp. baking powder
1/2 tsp. salt
1/2 c. butter or margarine, melted
1 egg
1/2 c. evaporated milk
1/2 c. sugar
1 c. brown sugar, firmly packed
1 c. regular oats, uncooked
1 c. pecans or walnuts, chopped
1 c. dates, chopped
1/4 c. mixed candied fruit, chopped
Glaze (recipe follows)
Red and green candied cherries

Combine first 3 ingredients in a large bowl. Add next 5 ingredients; beat until blended. Stir in oats. pecans, dates and candied fruit. Spread mixture in a greased 13" x 9" x 1" pan. Bake at 350 for 45-50 minutes. Cool. Drizzle with glaze. Cut into squares and decorate with cherries. Yield: 2 dozen.

Glaze:
1 c. sifted powdered sugar
2 Tbsp. milk
1/4 tsp. salt
1/2 tsp. vanilla extract

Combine all ingredients and stir until smooth. Yield: 1/2 cup.

Hint

Cool bar cookies on a rack until slightly warm before cutting into squares. After cutting, let them cool completely before removing from the pan.

SEVEN LAYER COOKIES

Melt 1 stick butter in 9" × 13" pan and add in the following order:
- 1 c. graham cracker crumbs, finely ground
- 1 c. flaked coconut
- 1 6-oz. package chocolate chips
- 1 6-oz. package butterscotch or peanut butter chips
- 1 can sweetened condensed milk
- 1 c. pecans, chopped

Bake at 350 for 30 minutes. Cool in pan and cut in small pieces. Makes about 40 squares.

🌲 🌲 🌲 🌲 🌲

CHOCOLATE CHERRY BARS

- 1 package Pillsbury Plus Dark Chocolate Cake Mix
- 1/3 c. margarine or butter, softened
- 1 egg
- 21-oz. can cherry fruit pie filling
- 1/2 c. powdered sugar
- 2 1/2 tsp. water

Heat oven to 350. In large bowl, combine cake mix and margarine at low speed. Reserve 1 c. crumbs for topping. To remaining mixture, blend in egg until well mixed. Press into ungreased 13" × 9" pan. Spoon pie filling over crust. Sprinkle with reserved crumbs. Bake at 350 for 30-40 minutes. Cool completely. Combine sugar and water. If thinner glaze is desired, stir in additional water a drop at a time. Drizzle over top. Loosen edges before cutting. Cut into squares. Makes 15 servings.

CHEWY CARAMEL BARS

32 Kraft caramels
2/3 c. evaporated milk
1 c. flour
3/4 c. quick oats
1/2 c. brown sugar
1/2 tsp. soda
1/4 tsp. salt
3/4 c. margarine
6 oz. semi-sweet chocolate pieces

Melt caramels with milk in covered double boiler or heavy sauce pan over low heat. Combine dry ingredients; cut in margarine until mixture resembles coarse crumbs. Reserve 1 cup. Press remaining mixture onto bottom of greased 9" × 13" pan. Bake at 350 for 12 minutes. Sprinkle chocolate pieces over baked crumbs. Spread caramel mixture evenly over chocolate pieces. Sprinkle remaining crumb mixture and continue baking for 20 minutes. Chill 2 hours. Cut into squares.

🌲   🌲   🌲   🌲   🌲

MERRY CHERRY CHEESECAKE BARS

Crust:
1/3 c. cold butter or margarine
1/3 c. brown sugar, firmly packed
1 c. flour

In small bowl, cut butter into chunks; add brown sugar and flour. Mix at low speed, then beat at medium speed, scraping sides of bowl often, until well mixed. Reserve 1/2 c. crumb mixture for topping; press remaining crumb mixture into 8" square pan. Bake near center of 350 oven for 10-12 minutes.

Filling:
8 oz. cream cheese, softened
1/4 c. sugar
1 egg
1 Tbsp. lemon juice
1/4 c. each glazed red and green cherries, chopped

Beat cream cheese, sugar, egg and lemon juice at medium speed until fluffy. Stir in chopped cherries. Spread filling over crust. Sprinkle with remaining crumb mixture. Continue baking for 18-20 minutes or until filling is set and top is lightly brown. Cool. Store in refrigerator. Makes 36 bars.

MARSHMALLOW FUDGE SQUARES

1/2 c. butter or margarine
2 squares unsweetened chocolate
1 c. flour
1 c. sugar
1 tsp. salt
1 tsp. vanilla
2 eggs
1/2 c. walnuts, chopped
1/2 c. semi-sweet chocolate chips
2 Tbsp. milk
30 large marshmallows

1. In a 1 quart saucepan over low heat, heat margarine and chocolate squares until melted and smooth, stirring occasionally. Remove from heat.
2. Preheat oven to 350. Grease 9" x 13" pan. In large bowl, measure flour, sugar, salt, vanilla and eggs. With mixer at low speed, beat ingredients until blended, occasionally scraping bowl. With spoon stir in nuts and chocolate mixture until blended. Spread mixture in pan. Bake 15 minutes.
3. Meanwhile, in small saucepan over low heat, heat semi-sweet chocolate pieces and milk until mixture is smooth. Remove saucepan from heat.
4. Remove baking pan from oven; arrange marshmallows in rows on top of baked layer in ban. Bake 5 minutes longer or until marshmallows are soft and puffed.
5. Remove pan to wire rack. With metal spatula, flatten marshmallows and spread to make an even layer. Drizzle melted chocolate mixture over marshmallow layer. Cool 30 minutes. Cover and refrigerate until cold and top is firm, about 2 hours. Cut. Store in tightly covered container in refrigerator to use up within 3 days. Makes 4 1/2 dozen squares. 75 calories per square.

Hint

Brownies should be slightly underbaked in the center. If cakelike brownies are desired, they are usually overbaked.

ALMOND JOY BARS

Blend together:
  1/2 c. soft butter or margarine
  2 c. graham cracker crumbs
  1/4 c. white sugar

1. Pat mixture into 9" × 13" buttered pan. Bake for 10 minutes at 350.
2. Sprinkle 2 c. coconut on top of crust mixture.
3. Pour 1 can Eagle Brand milk slowly over coconut. Bake for 10 minutes at 350.
4. Break 1 large economy size milk chocolate Hershey bar* into pieces over coconut mixture. Place back in oven for a minute to melt chocolate enough to spread. Then spread chocolate to cover coconut mixture. Cool in refrigerator and cut into small bars.

*8 small Hershey bars can be used instead.

🌲 🌲 🌲 🌲 🌲

SPEEDY LITTLE DEVILS

  1 Duncan Hines Deluxe II Devils Food cake mix
  1 stick margarine, melted
  3/4 c. creamy peanut butter
  1 7 1/2-oz. jar marshmallow creme

Combine melted margarine and dry cake mix. Reserve 1 1/2 c. of this topping for top crust. Pat remaining crumb mixture into ungreased 13" × 9" × 2" pan. Top that layer with combined peanut butter and marshmallow creme and spread evenly. Crumble remaining mixture over that. Bake 20 minutes at 350. Cool. Cut into 3 dozen bars.

11

TOFFEE BARS

1 c. butter or margarine
1 c. brown sugar
1 tsp. vanilla
2 c. sifted flour
6-oz. package semi-sweet chocolate chips
1 c. chopped walnuts

Thoroughly mix butter, brown sugar and vanilla. Add flour; mix well. Stir in chocolate chips and walnuts. Press into ungreased 15" × 10 1/2" × 1" jelly roll pan. Bake at 350° for 25 minutes or until brown. Cut into squares when cool. Makes 5 dozen.

🌲　🌲　🌲　🌲　🌲

DOUBLE CHOCOLATE CRUMBLE BARS

1/2 c. butter or margarine, softened
3/4 c. sugar
2 eggs
1 tsp. vanilla
3/4 c. flour
1/2 c. pecans, chopped
1 1/2 c. rice krispie cereal
2 Tbsp. cocoa powder
1/4 tsp. salt
1/4 tsp. baking powder
2 c. tiny marshmallows
1 6-oz. package semi-sweet chocolate chips
1 c. peanut butter

Cream butter and sugar; beat in eggs and vanilla. Mix together flour, nuts, cocoa, baking powder and salt; stir into egg mixture. Spread mixture into bottom of 13" × 9" × 2" pan; bake at 350 for 15-20 minutes or until bars test done. Sprinkle marshmallows on top; bake 3 minutes. Cool. In saucepan, combine chocolate chips and peanut butter. Cook and stir over low heat until chocolate is melted. Stir in cereal. Spread mixture on top of cooled bars. Chill; cut into bars. Makes 3-4 dozen. Store in refrigerator.

EXTRAVAGANZAS

Preheat oven to 400.

Crust:
   1 c. flour
   1/4 tsp. salt
   6 Tbsp. butter
   1 Tbsp. water

Combine flour and salt. Cut in butter until mixture is in coarse crumbs. Sprinkle in water and toss until pastry is just moist enough to hold together. Press into 9" square pan. Refrigerate 15 minutes. Bake 15 minutes.

Apricot layer:
   1 cup dried apricots
   1 1/4 c. water
   1/3 c. sugar

Meanwhile, simmer apricots, water and sugar in a small saucepan until apricots can be mashed with a fork, about 15 minutes. (A food processor or blender can be used.) Cool to room temperature.

Almond layer:
   1/2 c. butter, softened
   1 c. blanched almonds, ground
   1/2 c. sugar
   1 tsp. vanilla
   2 eggs
   1/8 tsp. almond extract

In large bowl at medium speed cream butter and sugar until fluffy. Add eggs, one at a time, and beat until well mixed. Stir in almonds and extracts.

Reduce oven heat to 350. Spread apricot mixture evenly over pastry. Cover with almond mixture. Smooth with spatula. Bake 30-35 minutes. Cool in pan. Drizzle with icing, if desired. Cut into small squares. Makes about 3 dozen.

Icing:
   1/2 c. powdered sugar
   1 Tbsp. milk
   1/2 tsp. vanilla

Stir until smooth and drizzle over bars.

MOCK TOFFEE

Soda crackers
2 sticks margarine
1 c. brown sugar
12-oz. package chocolate chips

Line cookie sheet with foil. Lay soda crackers on foil. Mix margarine and sugar in saucepan. Bring to full rolling boil. Pour boiling mixture over crackers. Bake 10 minutes in 350 oven.

Remove from oven and pour chocolate chips on top while still hot. As they melt, spread them around.

Place cookie sheet in refrigerator until cold. Break crackers into pieces and store in closed container in refrigerator.

CHOCOLATE-BUTTERSCOTCH SQUARES

2/3 c. butter, margarine or shortening, melted
2 1/4 c. brown sugar, packed
3 eggs
2 3/4 c. sifted flour
1/2 tsp. salt
2 1/2 tsp. baking powder
1 c. nuts, chopped
1 c. semi-sweet chocolate chips
1 tsp. vanilla

Mix butter and sugar thoroughly. Add eggs, one at a time, beating well after each addition. Add sifted dry ingredients, nuts, chocolate and vanilla. Spread into greased 15" × 10" × 1" pan. Bake at 350 about 35 minutes. Cut into about 40 squares while warm.

PECAN FINGERS

3/4 c. butter or margarine
3/4 c. powdered sugar
1 1/2 c. flour
2 eggs
1 c. brown sugar, packed
2 Tbsp. flour
1/2 tsp. baking powder
1/2 tsp. salt (or less)
1/2 tsp. vanilla
1 c. pecans, chopped

Heat oven to 350. Mix butter or margarine and powdered sugar thoroughly. Stir in 1 1/2 c. flour. Press and flatten mixture evenly with hand into ungreased 13" × 9" × 2" oblong pan. Bake 12 to 15 minutes. Mix remaining ingredients thoroughly; spread over baked layer. Bake 20 minutes; cool. Cut into bars.

🌲　🌲　🌲　🌲　🌲

FUDGE CHEESECAKE BARS

2 c. flour
1 1/2 c. butter or margarine, cut up
2/3 c. brown sugar, packed
1 package creamy fudge chocolate fudge frosting mix (for a two layer cake)
1 8-oz. package cream cheese, cut up
2 eggs
3/4 c. slivered almonds

1. Combine flour, butter and sugar; beat to resemble crumbs. Pat into 13" × 9" × 2" pan. Bake at 350 for 10-12 minutes. Remove and cool slightly.
2. Beat together next three ingredients until well blended. Pour over crust.
3. Sprinkle with slivered almonds.
4. Bake at 350 for 25-30 minutes. Cool and cut into bars.

FUDGE BROWNIES

Melt over low heat:
   1 cube butter
   2 squares baking chocolate
Add and beat well:
   1 c. sugar
Beat in:
   2 whole eggs
Add and mix well:
   1/2 c. flour
   pinch of salt
   1 tsp. vanilla
   1/2 c. chopped nuts (optional)
Pour into greased 8" x 8" pan. Bake at 350 for 25-30 minutes.

FUDGE-NUT LAYER BARS

   1 12-oz. package semi-sweet chocolate chips
   1 8-oz. package cream cheese, cubed
   2/3 c. evaporated milk
   1 c. walnuts, chopped
In saucepan, combine chocolate chips, cream cheese and evaporated milk. Stir over low heat until smooth. Stir in nuts.
   1 1/2 c. sugar
   1/2 c. margarine
   2 eggs
   1/2 tsp. vanilla
   3 c. flour
   1 tsp. baking powder
   1/2 tsp. salt
Cream sugar and margarine until light and fluffy. Blend in eggs and vanilla. Add remaining ingredients. Mix well. Press 1/2 mixture on bottom of 13" x 9" baking pan.
Spread chocolate mixture over crust. Sprinkle with remaining crust mixture. Press lightly. Bake at 375 for 30 minutes. Cool. Cut into bars.

FUDGY OATMEAL WHEAT GERM BROWNIES

These brownies have a pleasant nutty flavor and chewy texture.

    1 6-oz. package semi-sweet chocolate pieces
    5 Tbsp. butter
    3/4 c. plus 2 Tbsp. quick-cooking oats
    1/4 c. toasted wheat germ
    1/3 c. nonfat dry milk powder
    1/2 tsp. baking powder
    1/2 tsp. salt
    1/2 c. walnuts, chopped
    2 eggs
    1/4 c. brown sugar, firmly packed
    1/4 c. granulated sugar
    1 tsp. vanilla

Preheat oven to 350. Grease 8" × 8" × 2" pan. Melt chocolate with butter in small heavy saucepan over very low heat or in top of double boiler over simmering water. Remove from heat; blend thoroughly. Reserve. Combine oats, wheat germ, nonfat dry milk, baking powder, salt and walnuts in medium-size bowl; mix well. Reserve. Beat eggs in medium bowl until light. Gradually beat in brown and granulated sugars and vanilla until mixture is thick. Stir in reserved chocolate mixture; fold in reserved oat mixture. Spread batter into prepared baking pan. Bake in preheated 350 oven for 20-25 minutes or until wooden pick inserted in center comes out barely moist and top is crisp and edges are firm. Cool completely in pan on wire rack. Cover with aluminum foil; refrigerate overnight. Cut into squares.

Microwave directions: Combine chocolate and butter in 4 c. glass container. Microwave, uncovered, at full power for 1 1/2 minutes. Stir until all the chocolate is melted. Prepare brownie batter as directed above. Spread into greased 8" × 8" × 2" microwave-safe baking dish. Place dish on microwave oven rack or on inverted saucer. Microwave, uncovered, at full power for 6 minutes. Center should look moist but set. Cool as directed above.

Chocolate Frosting:
    1 1/2 c. sugar
    6 Tbsp. margarine
    6 Tbsp. milk
    1/2 c. chocolate chips
    1 tsp. vanilla

Combine and bring to a rolling boil only 30 seconds. Add chocolate chips and vanilla. Beat until dissolved. Spread immediately.

GLAZED ORANGE-SHORTBREAD SQUARES

3 c. flour, sifted
1/2 c. cornstarch
1 c. sugar
Grated rind of 1 orange
1/4 tsp. salt
1 c. butter or margarine
1/3 c. orange juice
Orange Glaze
2 squares unsweetened chocolate

Put first 5 ingredients into bowl and mix well. Cut in butter until particles are very fine. Add orange juice and toss to mix. Gather mixture together and work quickly with hands until crumbs form a dough. With lightly floured fingertips, press evenly onto bottom of lightly buttered 15" x 10" x 1" pan. Bake in 350 oven for 25 minutes or until golden brown. Cool and spread glaze*. Let set. Melt chocolate over hot water (microwave). Cool and pour into small cone made of double waxed paper, leaving 1/16" opening. Squeeze out onto glaze in desired pattern. Let stand until firm, then cut into 48 squares. Store airtight in cool place. Fairly good keepers and shippers. NOTE: if preferred, omit cone and drizzle chocolate over glaze with teaspoon.

*Orange glaze:
    2 c. confectioners' sugar
    1/4 c. orange juice

ENGLISH TOFFEE COOKIES

Preheat oven to 350. Grease large cookie sheet with butter, and spread with 1 box regular graham crackers sectioned where perforated. In saucepan combine and boil 3 minutes:
    1 c. butter
    1/2 c. brown sugar
    1/2 c. chopped nuts (pecans preferred)
Pour over graham crackers on cookie sheet and bake 10 minutes. Remove and immediately top with 12 oz. semi-sweet chocolate chips (or mix 6 oz. butterscotch and 6 oz. chocolate chips). They will melt. Spread with knife. Let cool. Break apart or cut. Approximately 25 pieces.

ORANGE-NUT BARS

3 eggs
1 6-oz. can frozen orange
   juice concentrate
1 c. sugar
2 c. graham cracker crumbs
1 tsp. baking powder
1/4 tsp. salt
1 c. nuts, chopped
1 8-oz. package pitted
   dates, chopped
1 tsp. vanilla

1. Preheat oven to 350.
2. Grease and lightly flour a 9-inch square pan.
3. Beat the eggs until light and fluffy. Beat in the orange juice concentrate.
4. Stir in the remaining ingredients and mix well.
5. Spoon the mixture onto the prepared pan. Bake at 350 for 50 minutes.
6. Remove from oven and cool in the pan on a rack. Frost with Orange Icing and cut into bars. Makes 21-28.

Orange Icing:
   1 1/4 c. confectioners' sugar
   2 1/2 Tbsp. orange juice
Beat until smooth and ready to spread.

🌲 🌲 🌲 🌲 🌲

DATE-NUT DREAM SQUARES

1 package 2-layer yellow
   cake mix
1 3 3/4-oz. package instant
   coconut cream pudding mix
1/2 c. butter or margarine,
   softened
1 slightly beaten egg
1/2 c. all-purpose flour
1/2 c. brown sugar, packed
1/4 c. water
2 eggs
1 tsp. vanilla
1/8 tsp. salt
1 8-oz. package pitted
   dates, snipped
1/2 c. walnuts, chopped

In large mixer bowl, combine cake, pudding mix, butter and first egg. Beat at low speed just until crumbly, about 1 minute. Reserve 1/2 c. crumb mixture. Press remaining mixture into bottom of greased 9" × 13" pan. Bake at 350 for 15 minutes. Meanwhile, in same bowl combine flour, brown sugar, water, the remaining egg, vanilla and salt; beat until smooth. Stir in dates and nuts. Carefully spread over base. Sprinkle with reserved crumbs. Bake in 350 oven for 20 minutes. Cut into squares. Serve with whipped cream, if desired. Makes 12 servings.

CRUNCH-TOP APPLESAUCE BARS

1 1/4 c. sugar
1 c. applesauce
1/2 c. shortening
2 c. sifted flour
1 tsp. soda
1 1/2 tsp. cinnamon
1 tsp. nutmeg
dash of cloves
1/4 tsp. salt
1/2 c. seedless raisins
1/2 c. walnuts, chopped
1 tsp. vanilla
2/3 c. corn flakes, crushed
2 Tbsp. butter, softened

Combine 1 cup sugar and applesauce; add shortening and blend. Sift together flour, soda, spices and salt; add to applesauce mixture. Stir until smooth. Stir in raisins, 1/4 c. coarsely chopped nuts and vanilla. Spread batter into greased 15 1/2" × 10 1/2" × 1" jelly roll pan. Combine cornflakes, remaining sugar, remaining nuts and butter; sprinkle over batter. Bake in 350 oven for 30 minutes or until done. Cool; cut into bars. Yield: 32 bars.

🌲　🌲　🌲　🌲　🌲

CHEESE CRUNCHERS

12-oz. package butterscotch chips
6 Tbsp. butter
2 c. graham cracker crumbs
2 c. nuts, chopped
2 8-oz. packages cream cheese, softened
1/2 c. sugar
4 eggs
1/4 c. unsifted flour
2 Tbsp. lemon juice

Combine chips and butter over hot water. Heat until melted and smooth. Transfer to large bowl; stir in graham cracker crumbs and nuts. Stir until mixture forms small crumbs. Reserve 2 c. crumb mixture for topping. Press remaining mixture into 15" × 10" baking pan. Bake at 350 for 12 minutes.

In large bowl combine cream cheese and sugar; beat until creamy. Add eggs, one at a time. Blend in flour and lemon juice. Pour over hot crust. Sprinkle top with reserved crumbs. Bake at 350 for 25 minutes. Cool and cut into bars. Makes 75.

CHERRY SQUARES

1 1/4 c. flour
2 Tbsp. sugar
1/2 c. butter or margarine
pinch of salt

Cream butter; add sugar and flour. Pat into 7" × 11" pan. Bake 5 minutes at 350.

1 c. brown sugar
2 egg, beaten
3/4 c. nuts, chopped
3/4 c. glazed cherries
2 Tbsp. flour
1/2 tsp. baking powder
1/4 tsp. salt

Mix. Spread mixture over pastry and bake for 25 minutes at 350.

Buttercream Frosting:
1/2 c. margarine
2 c. powdered sugar
3 Tbsp. milk
1 tsp. vanilla

Mix until smooth. Spread over cooled bars.

🌲 🌲 🌲 🌲 🌲

CHINESE CHEWS

3/4 c. flour
1 c. sugar
1 tsp. baking powder
1/4 tsp. salt
1 c. dates, chopped
1 c. walnuts, chopped
3 eggs, well beaten
confectioners' sugar

Sift dry ingredients. Stir in dates, walnuts and eggs. Pour into greased and floured 15" × 10" × 1" jelly roll pan. Bake at 350 for 15 minutes. While warm, cut into bars. Cool; remove from pans. Roll in sifted confectioners' sugar. Makes 3 dozen.

PEANUT BUTTER MELTAWAYS

Crust:
- 1 1/4 c. flour
- 3/4 tsp. baking soda
- 1/2 tsp. baking powder
- 1/4 tsp. salt
- 1/2 c. butter or margarine at room temperature
- 1/2 c. smooth peanut butter
- 1 c. sugar
- 1 large egg
- 2 Tbsp. water

Topping:
- 26 caramels
- 1/4 c. heavy cream
- 1 tsp. vanilla
- 1/2 c. semi-sweet chocolate chips
- 1/3 c. unsalted peanuts, chopped

Heat oven to 375. Grease a 9" × 13" baking pan. To make crust, mix flour, baking soda, baking powder and salt. In a large bowl, beat butter, peanut butter and sugar with electric mixer until fluffy. Beat in egg and water. Stir in flour mixture until well blended. Spread into prepared baking pan. Bake for 15-20 minutes until brown and center is firm to touch. Cool in pan on rack. To make topping, heat caramels and heavy cream in a medium-size saucepan over low heat until caramels melt and mixture is smooth, stirring occasionally. Remove from heat; stir in vanilla. Carefully spread over cooled crust. Sprinkle with peanuts; press lightly onto topping. Cool in pan on rack. Refrigerate until firm enough to cut into 54 bars.

🌲 🌲 🌲 🌲 🌲

BUTTERFINGER BARS

- 1 c. brown sugar
- 1/2 c. white sugar
- 1 c. margarine
- 4 c. oatmeal
- 6 oz. chocolate chips
- 3/4 c. peanut butter

Mix and press into a 9" × 13" pan. Bake for 30 minutes at 350. Melt chocolate chips and peanut butter. Spread over bars when baked.

HIGH-ALTITUDE MARBLED BROWNIES

FABULOUS! Chocolate lovers will go bonkers over these!

1 stick butter or margarine
1/3 c. unsweetened cocoa
3 eggs
1 c. plus 2 Tbsp. sugar
1 tsp. vanilla
1/2 c. unsifted flour
1/2 tsp. baking powder
1/4 tsp. salt
1 c. peanut butter chips
1 3-oz. package cream cheese, softened

Melt butter in small saucepan. Remove from heat and stir in cocoa; set aside. Beat two of the eggs in small mixing bowl until foamy. Gradually add one cup sugar and vanilla. Combine flour, baking powder and salt. Blend into egg mixture. Add chocolate mixture and half of the peanut butter chips, blending well. Reserve 1/2 cup of the mixture.

Spread remaining mixture into greased 9" square pan. Melt remaining peanut butter chips over hot water. Combine cream cheese, remaining sugar and melted peanut butter chips. Beat until smooth. Add remaining egg. Beat until fluffy. Spread cream cheese mixture evenly over chocolate mixture in pan. Drop reserved chocolate-peanut butter mixture by spoonfuls onto cream cheese. Gently swirl top of batter with knife to marble. Bake in 350 oven for 40-45 minutes or until brownie begins to pull away from edges of pan. Cool and cut into squares. Makes 16 brownies.

🌲 🌲 🌲 🌲 🌲

FRUITCAKE BARS

6 Tbsp. butter or margarine
4 c. vanilla wafer crumbs
3/4 c. green candied cherries, halved
3/4 c. red candied cherries, halved
1/2 c. candied pineapple, chopped
3/4 c. dates, chopped
1 c. pecans, whole or chopped
1 14-oz. can sweetened condensed milk
1/4 c. bourbon

In a saucepan melt butter or margarine; pour into 15" x 10" x 1" baking pan. Sprinkle vanilla wafer crumbs evenly on top. Arrange fruits and nuts evenly over crumb mixture; press down gently. Combine the sweetened condensed milk and bourbon; pour evenly over top. Bake in 350 oven for 20-25 minutes. Remove from oven and cool completely. Cut into squares. Makes 60.

TOFFEE BARS II

Cream:
  1 c. butter
  1 c. brown sugar
Add:
  1 tsp. vanilla
  1 egg yolk
Blend in:
  2 c. flour sifted with 1/4 tsp. salt
Spread thinly onto a buttered cookie sheet. Bake at 350 for 20 minutes. Remove from oven and, while hot, spread with 1 large Hershey bar. Sprinkle with nuts. Cut into squares.

🌲　🌲　🌲　🌲　🌲

ZEBRAS

  2 c. flour
  1 tsp. baking powder
  1 1/2 c. semi-sweet chocolate chips
  1 c. butter or margarine at room temperature
  1 c. light brown sugar, packed
  2 large eggs
  1 tsp. vanilla
  3/4 c. walnuts, coarsely chopped
Preheat oven to 350. Grease 13" × 9" pan. Line with foil; grease and sprinkle with flour. Mix flour and baking powder. Melt 1 c. chocolate chips in saucepan over low hear, stirring often. Remove from heat; cool slightly. In bowl, beat butter and sugar with electric mixer until fluffy. Beat in eggs, one at a time, beating well after each addition. Beat in vanilla. Stir in flour mixture. Transfer half of the batter to another bowl. Stir melted chocolate into one portion. Spread chocolate batter into prepared pan. Drop tablespoons of the remaining batter over chocolate layer. Spread carefully in an even layer. Sprinkle with remaining 1/2 c. chocolate chips and walnuts. Bake for 30-35 minutes until edges begin to pull away from sides of pan. Cool in pan on rack. Makes 24 bars.

CUPID'S BAIT

2 c. brown sugar
1 1/2 Tbsp. cocoa
1/4 tsp. salt
2 Tbsp. cheddar cheese, grated
1 tsp. vanilla
1/2 c. margarine, melted
2 eggs, unbeaten
1 1/4 c. flour
1 tsp. baking powder
1 c. nuts, chopped

Mix in order of ingredients listed. Spread into buttered 8" × 8" pan and bake at 375 for 25 minutes. Cool for 1-2 minutes then cut into squares while still hot and roll each square in powdered sugar.

♠ ♠ ♠ ♠ ♠

GRASSHOPPER SQUARES

Base:
  Cream:
    3/4 c. powdered sugar
    3/4 c. margarine or butter
  Add:
    2 oz. unsweetened chocolate, melted
  Blend:
    1 1/2 c. flour
    1/2 tsp. baking powder
    1/4 tsp. salt
    1 Tbsp. milk
    1/4 tsp. mint extract

Filling:
  Cream:
    4 c. powdered sugar
    3 oz. package cream cheese
    1/4 c. margarine or butter
    3 Tbsp. milk
    1 tsp. vanilla
    1/4 tsp. mint extract
    6 drops green food coloring
    Chocolate decorator candies

Bake at 325 for 20-25 minutes in 9" × 13" greased pan. Makes 48 bars.

PUMPKIN CHEESECAKE BARS

1 16-oz. package Betty Crocker Golden Pound Cake Mix
3 eggs
2 Tbsp. margarine, melted
4 tsp. pumpkin pie spice
1 8-oz. package cream cheese, softened
1 14-oz. can Eagle brand Sweetened Condensed milk
1 16-oz. can pumpkin (about 2 cups)
1/2 tsp. salt
1 c. nuts, chopped

Preheat oven to 350.

Combine cake mix, 1 egg, margarine and 2 tsp. pumpkin pie spice until crumbly. Pat into bottom of 15" × 10" × 1" jelly roll pan.

Beat cream cheese until fluffy. Add milk, remaining 2 eggs, remaining 2 tsp. pumpkin pie spice and salt. Pour over crust. Sprinkle nuts on top.

Bake 30-35 minutes or until set. Cool, chill and cut into bars. Store in refrigerator. Makes 48 bars.

CHOCOLATE PECAN PIE BARS

1 1/4 c. all-purpose flour
1/4 c. granulated sugar
1/2 tsp. baking powder
1/2 tsp. ground cinnamon
1/2 c. butter or margarine
1 c. pecans, finely chopped
1/4 c. butter or margarine
1 1-oz. square semi-sweet chocolate
3 eggs, beaten
1 1/4 c. brown sugar, packed
2 Tbsp. bourbon or water
1 tsp. vanilla

In a mixing bowl stir together flour, sugar, baking powder and cinnamon. Cut in 1/2 c. butter until mixture resembles coarse crumbs. Stir in pecans. Press into bottom of ungreased 13" × 9" baking pan. Bake in 350 oven for 10 minutes.

Meanwhile, in a small saucepan combine the 1/4 c. butter and chocolate; heat and stir over low heat until chocolate is melted. In a small mixing bowl combine the eggs, brown sugar, bourbon or water, and vanilla. Stir mixture until well blended; pour over crust. Return to oven. Bake 20 minutes. Cool. Cut into bars. Makes 36.

COOKIE BRITTLE

1 c. unsalted butter, room temperature
1 1/2 tsp. vanilla
1 tsp. salt
2 c. unbleached flour, sifted
1 c. sugar
1 7.8-oz. package Heath Bits O Brickle candy

Preheat oven to 375. Combine butter, vanilla and salt in medium bowl and beat with electric mixer until fluffy. Add flour, sugar and candy; blend well. Press mixture into 15" × 11" jelly roll pan. Cover with waxed paper and flatten with rolling pin. Discard paper. Bake until golden brown, about 25 minutes. Cut brittle into squares, or let cool and break into pieces.

🌲 🌲 🌲 🌲 🌲

CRUNCHY PEANUT ALMOND BARS

1 package Pillsbury Plus Yellow Cake Mix
1/2 c. margarine or butter, softened
2 eggs
1 c. brown sugar, firmly packed
1/2 tsp. salt
3 Tbsp. peanut butter
1/2 tsp. vanilla
7.8-oz. package almond brickle baking chips
1 c. peanuts, chopped

Preheat oven to 350. Combine cake mix and margarine; stir until crumbly. Reserve 1/2 c. crumb mixture for topping; press remaining crumbs into ungreased 13" × 9" pan. Bake 10 minutes.
In small bowl, beat eggs until frothy. Add brown sugar, salt, peanut butter and vanilla; beat 2 minutes at medium speed. Stir in reserved crumbs, almond brickle baking chips and peanuts; spread over crumb crust.
Bake at 350 for 20-25 minutes or until golden brown. (Topping will be soft in center). Cool completely. Cut into bars. Makes 2-3 dozen bars.

ORANGE LIQUEUR BROWNIES

3/4 c. butter or margarine
6 oz. unsweetened chocolate
4 eggs
4 tsp. orange-flavored liqueur
1 tsp. vanilla
2 c. sugar
1 c. all-purpose or unbleached flour

Heat oven to 350. Lightly grease 13" x 9" pan. In saucepan over low heat, melt butter and chocolate, stirring constantly. Cool.

In large bowl, beat eggs, liqueur and vanilla at high speed until thick and lemon colored. Gradually add sugar, beating until fluffy. Add chocolate mixture. Fold in flour. Spread into pan. Bake 25-35 minutes and cool.

Frosting:
1/2 c. butter, softened
2 c. powdered sugar
1/8 tsp. salt
3 Tbsp. orange-flavored liqueur
1/2 tsp. vanilla

In small bowl, beat butter and add remaining frosting ingredients. Beat until smooth and creamy. Spread over cooled brownies.

Glaze:
1 oz. unsweetened chocolate
1 tsp. butter

Melt chocolate and butter, stirring until well blended. Drizzle over frosted brownies. Refrigerate. Makes 48 bars.

🌲 🌲 🌲 🌲 🌲

ENGLISH TOFFEE BARS

1/2 c. butter
1/2 c. shortening
1 c. brown sugar
1 egg yolk
1 tsp. vanilla
1/2 tsp. salt
2 c. flour, sifted
1/2 c. nuts, chopped
6 oz. milk chocolate chips

Cream butter, shortening, sugar and egg yolk. Stir in vanilla, salt and flour. Pat into 15" x 10" x 1" pan. Bake at 325 for 15-25 minutes (light brown). Sprinkle with chips. Place in oven until melted. Spread chocolate over top and sprinkle with nuts. Cut into bars.

MARSHMALLOW BARS

Melt in heavy saucepan, stirring constantly, and cool:
- 1/2 c. butterscotch (or peanut butter) bits
- 1/4 c. margarine

Add and mix well:
- 3/4 c. flour
- 1/3 c. brown sugar
- 1 tsp. baking powder
- 1/4 tsp. salt
- 1/2 tsp. burnt sugar flavoring
- 1 egg

Fold in:
- 1 c. miniature marshmallows
- 1 c. chocolate bits
- 1/3 c. nuts, chopped

Spread into greased 8" square pan. Bake in a 350 oven 20-25 minutes. Do not overbake. Center will be jiggly, but becomes firm. When cool, cut into small squares. Makes approximately 2 dozen bars.

HONEY FRUIT BARS

- 1 1/3 c. all-purpose flour, sifted
- 1 tsp. baking powder
- 1/4 tsp. salt
- 3 eggs
- 1 c. honey
- 1 tsp. vanilla
- 1 3/4 c. dates, pitted and chopped
- 1 c. nuts, chopped
- 1/2 c. candied cherries, halved

Preheat oven to 350. Grease a 13" × 9" × 2" pan. Sift together flour, baking powder and salt. Beat eggs. Add honey and vanilla. Mix well. Add flour mixture, dates, nuts and cherries. Mix well. Spread in pan. Bake 45 minutes or until browned. Cool in pan on wire rack. Cut in 3" × 1" bars. Roll in confectioners' sugar. Makes 39 bars. Store in airtight container. Can be frozen. Good keepers, shippers.

FROSTED DELIGHTS

3/4 c. shortening (can use half butter or margarine, softened)
3/4 c. powdered sugar
1 1/2 c. flour

Heat oven to 350. Cream shortening/butter and powdered sugar. Blend in flour. Will make a stiff dough (if too stiff, add a few drops of water or milk and blend). Press dough evenly over bottom of ungreased 13" x 9" x 2" pan. Bake approximately 10-12 minutes.

Meanwhile:
3 eggs, beaten
1 1/2 c. brown sugar, packed
3 Tbsp. flour
3/4 tsp. baking powder
1/2 tsp. salt
1 tsp. vanilla
1 c. pecans, chopped
1 c. flaked coconut

Beat eggs; add remaining ingredients; spread over hot baked layer and bake 20 minutes longer. Cool to warm and spread with lemon glaze (recipe follows). Cool. Cut into bars, whatever size your family likes. A good keeper in tins.

Lemon Glaze:
1 1/2 c. powdered sugar
2 Tbsp. butter or margarine, melted
3-4 Tbsp. lemon juice, fresh or reconstituted
1 tsp. lemon rind (optional)

Mix all ingredients together until smooth enough to spread. Spread over warm cookies in pan.

🌲 🌲 🌲 🌲 🌲

SCOTCH SHORTBREAD

Preheat oven to 325.
Cream:
1 c. butter
Sift together:
2 c. all-purpose flour, sifted
1/2 c. confectioners' sugar, sifted
1/4 tsp. salt

Blend the dry ingredients into the butter. Work dough with your hands and pat evenly into ungreased 9" x 9" pan. Pierce with a fork through the dough about every half inch. Bake for 25-30 minutes. Cut into squares while warm. Squares should not be more than 1 1/2" x 1 1/2" —even 1" squares are not too small.

CHERRY CHEESE BARS

Crust:
  1 c. walnuts, divided
  1 1/4 c. flour, unsifted
  1/2 c. brown sugar, firmly packed
  1/2 c. Butter Flavor Crisco
  1/2 c. flake coconut

Preheat oven to 350. Grease bottom of 13" × 9" × 2" pan. Chop 1/2 c. walnuts coarsely for topping. Set aside. Chop remaining 1/2 c. finely. For crust, combine flour and brown sugar. Cut in Butter Flavor Crisco until fine crumbs form. Add 1/2 c. finely chopped nuts and coconut. Mix well. Remove 1/2 c. and set aside. Press remaining crumbs onto bottom of greased pan. Bake at 350 for 12-15 minutes, until edges are lightly browned.

Filling:
  1 8-oz. package cream cheese, softened
  1/3 c. granulated sugar
  1 egg
  1 tsp. vanilla
  1 21-oz. can regular or light cherry pie filling

Beat cream cheese, granulated sugar, egg and vanilla until smooth. Spread over hot baked crust. Return to oven. Bake 10 minutes longer. Spread cherry pie filling over cheese layer. Combine reserved coarsely chopped nuts and reserved crumbs. Sprinkle evenly over cherries. Return to oven. Bake 15 minutes longer. Cool. Cut into 24 bars.

🌲 🌲 🌲 🌲 🌲

COCONUT SQUARES

  1/4 c. flour
  1/2 c. butter
  3 Tbsp. cold water
  2 large eggs
  1/2 c. sugar
  7-oz. package coconut
  1/2 c. raspberry preserves

In a medium bowl cut butter into flour until size of large peas. Sprinkle with water. Mix lightly. Form into a ball. Press into ungreased 9" × 9" pan. Bake in preheated 425 oven for 20 minutes. Remove. Turn oven to 375. Beat eggs; add sugar and coconut. Spread preserves over pastry leaving 1/4" space on edges. Carefully spread coconut mixture over preserves. Bake for about 25 minutes.

CREAM CHEESE CHOCOLATE BARS

1 package Pillsbury Plus Devil's Food Cake Mix
1 1/4 c. Quick Cooking rolled oats
1/2 c. margarine or butter, softened
1 egg
1/2 c. pecans, chopped
1/4 c. brown sugar, firmly packed

Heat oven to 350. Grease 13" x 9" x 2" pan. In large bowl, combine cake mix, 1 c. oats and 6 Tbsp. margarine at low speed until crumbly. Reserve 1 c. crumbs. To remaining crumbs, blend in egg. Press into prepared pan. Bake for 12 minutes. Meanwhile, to reserved crumbs, add remaining 1/4 c. oats, 2 Tbsp. margarine, nuts and brown sugar. Beat until well mixed.

Filling:
1/3 c. sugar
1 egg
8-oz. package cream cheese, softened

In small bowl, blend all filling ingredients until smooth. Remove base from oven; let stand 10 minutes. Spread with filling. Sprinkle with reserved crumbs. Return to oven and bake 15 minutes. Cool completely. Cut into bars or squares.

🌲 🌲 🌲 🌲 🌲

CHOCOLATE PEPPERMINT BARS

1 12-oz. package chocolate chips
2 14-oz. cans Eagle Brand condensed milk
1 1/2 + 4 Tbsp. butter
1 tsp. peppermint extract
2 1/2 c. brown sugar, firmly packed
2 eggs
3 c. flour
3 c. quick oatmeal
1 1/2 c. nuts, chopped
2/3 c. crushed hard peppermint candy (optional)

Preheat oven to 350. In heavy saucepan, over low heat, melt chips with Eagle Brand milk and 4 Tbsp. butter; remove from heat. Add extract; set aside. In large bowl, beat remaining butter with sugar until fluffy; beat in egg. Add flour and oats; mix well. With floured hands, press 2/3 oat mixture into 2 greased 15" x 10" jelly roll pans; spread chocolate mixture evenly on top. Add nuts to remaining oat mixture; crumble evenly over chocolate. Sprinkle with peppermint candy. Bake for 15-18 minutes. Cool thoroughly before cutting.

RASPBERRY BARS II

1 1/4 c. flour, sifted
1/2 tsp. salt
1 tsp. sugar
1 tsp. baking powder
1/2 c. butter
1 egg yolk
2 Tbsp. Brandy or milk
3/4 c. raspberry jam
2 eggs
2 tsp. vanilla
6 Tbsp. butter, melted
2 1/2 c. flaked coconut
1 1 /2 c. sugar

Sift flour, salt, 1 tsp. sugar and baking powder. Blend in 1/2 c. butter, egg yolk and Brandy. Pat into buttered 7" × 11" × 2" pan. Spread with jam. Beat 2 eggs until thick and lemon colored. Beat in 1 1/2 c. sugar, vanilla and melted butter. Add coconut then spoon over jam. Bake at 350 for 35 minutes. Makes approximately 3 dozen.

COFFEE-DATE BARS

1 1/4 c. flour, sifted
2 Tbsp. instant coffee
2 tsp. baking powder
1/4 tsp. salt
3 eggs
1 c. sugar
1/2 c. dates, finely chopped
1/2 c. walnuts, coarsely chopped

Measure flour, instant coffee, baking powder and salt into sifter.
Beat eggs until light in a medium-sized bowl; beat in sugar slowly. Continue beating until thick; stir in dates and walnuts. Sift flour mixture and fold into egg mixture. Spread into a greased 9" × 13" × 2" pan. Bake at 350 for 35 minutes or until a wooden pick inserted in center comes out clean. Cool completely in pan on wire rack; cut into bars. Makes 3 dozen bars.

BUTTER PECAN TURTLES

Crust:
  2 c. flour
  1 c. brown sugar
  1/2 c. butter

Caramel layer:
  2/3 c. butter
  1/2 c. brown sugar
  1 c. pecan halves
  1 c. milk chocolate chips

Preheat oven to 350. Mix crust at medium speed 2-3 minutes until texture is fine. Pat firmly into 9" x 13" x 2" pan; sprinkle pecans over unbaked crust. Put brown sugar and butter in medium pan over medium heat, stirring constantly until surface begins to boil. Boil 1/2-1 minute. Pour over pecans. Bake at 350 for 18-20 minutes or until caramel layer is bubbly and crust is light brown. Remove from oven. Sprinkle with chips. After 2-3 minutes swirl over surface.

🌲 🌲 🌲 🌲 🌲

LEANNE'S BUTTER COOKIE SQUARES

  1 c. REAL butter
  1 c. granulated sugar
  1 tsp. vanilla
  1 egg yolk (white to be used later)
  1 tsp. salt
  2 c. flour
  chopped pecans

Mix first six ingredients and spread onto 16 1/2" x 11" jelly roll pan that has been sprayed with Baker's Joy. Press dough into place with heal of hand. Whip egg white and spread on top. Sprinkle with chopped pecans and press lightly into place. Bake until light golden brown. Remove from oven and cut into squares or desired size immediately. Gently remove from pan to rack to cool. Enjoy!!

CHOCOLATE-CHERRY SQUARES

1 c. all-purpose flour
1/3 c. butter or margarine
1/2 c. light brown sugar, packed
1/2 c. nuts, chopped
Filling
Red candied cherries, halved

Heat oven to 350. In large mixer bowl, combine flour, butter and brown sugar. Blend on low speed to form fine crumbs, about 2-3 minutes. Stir in nuts. Reserve 3/4 c. crumb mixture for topping; pat remaining crumbs into ungreased 9" × 13" × 2" pan. Bake 10 minutes or until lightly browned. Meanwhile, prepare filling; spread over warm crust. Sprinkle with reserved crumb mixture; garnish with cherry halves. Return to oven; bake 25 minutes or until lightly browned. Cool. Cut into squares. Store, covered, in refrigerator. Makes about 3 dozen squares.

Filling:
1 8-oz. package cream cheese, softened
1/2 c. sugar
1/3 c. cocoa
1/4 c. milk
1 egg
1/4 tsp. vanilla extract
1/4 c. red candied cherries, chopped

In small mixer bowl combine cream cheese and sugar; beat until fluffy. Add cocoa, milk, egg and vanilla; beat until smooth. Fold in cherries.

🌲　🌲　🌲　🌲　🌲

CARAMEL RIBBON BARS

1 package yellow cake mix (two-layer size)
1/2 c. walnuts, chopped
1 5-oz. can evaporated milk
1/4 c. butter or margarine, melted
1/2 c. semi-sweet chocolate pieces
1/2 c. caramel topping

In a mixing bowl, combine dry cake mix and walnuts. Stir in evaporated milk and melted margarine or butter. Spread about half of the cake mixture in a greased 13" × 9" × 2" pan. Bake at 350 for 10 minutes. Remove from oven and sprinkle chocolate pieces over hot crust. Drizzle with caramel topping. Drop remaining cake mixture by teaspoon over all. Bake 20-25 minutes more. Cool on wire rack. While still warm, loosen sides and cut into bars. Makes 36 bars.

CHOCOLATE NUGGET BAR

First layer:
    11 1/2-oz. package milk chocolate chips
    1/2 c. butterscotch chips
    1/2 c. creamy peanut butter
Melt all ingredients. Stir well and spread half of mixture into buttered 9" × 13" pan. Cool. Reserve other half for fourth layer.

Second layer:
    1 c. sugar
    1/4 c. whole milk
    4 Tbsp. margarine
    1/4 c. marshmallow creme
    1 tsp. vanilla extract
    2 c. dry roasted peanuts
Boil sugar, milk and margarine for 5 minutes. Add marshmallow creme and vanilla. Pour over bottom layer and sprinkle with roasted nuts.

Third layer:
    1 pound or 14 oz. bag caramels
    2 Tbsp. hot water
Add hot water to caramels and melt in saucepan or microwave. Drizzle over peanuts.

Fourth layer:
    Spread reserved half of chocolate mixture on top. Cool completely and cut into squares.

ENGLISH MATRIMONIALS

Mix together:
    1 1/2 c. flour
    1 c. brown sugar
    1 1/4 c. oatmeal
Work in until crumbly.
    3/4 c. butter or margarine
Press 1/2 of mixture into 8" × 8" greased baking dish.
Spread with:
    1 c. raspberry jam
    1 c. walnuts
Press rest of oatmeal mixture on top. Bake at 350 for 40-45 minutes or until golden.

ULTIMATE CHOCOLATE BROWNIES

3/4 c. cocoa
1/2 tsp. baking soda
2/3 c. butter or margarine, melted and divided
1/2 c. boiling water
2 c. sugar
2 eggs
1 1/3 c. flour
1 tsp. vanilla
1/4 tsp. salt
1 c. semi-sweet chocolate chips
1 bowl Buttercream Frosting

Heat oven to 350. Grease 9" × 13" × 2" pan or 2 8" × 8" pans. In medium bowl combine cocoa and baking soda. Blend in 1/3 c. melted butter. Add boiling water; stir until mixture thickens. Stir in sugar, eggs and remaining 1/3 c. melted butter; stir until smooth. Add flour, vanilla and salt; blend completely. Stir in chocolate chips. Pour into pan. Bake for 35-40 minutes or until brownies begin to pull away from sides of pan. Cool completely in pan; spread with frosting. Cut into squares. Makes about 3 dozen brownies.

Frosting:
6 Tbsp. butter or margarine, softened
1/2 c. cocoa
2 2/3 c. powdered sugar
1/3 c. milk
1 tsp. vanilla extract

In small mixer bowl cream butter. Add cocoa and powdered sugar alternately with milk; beat to spreading consistency (additional milk may be needed). Blend in vanilla. Makes about 2 cups. Spread over brownies and decorate with chocolate chips and crushed peppermint sticks.

Hint

Bake brownies until edges begin to pull away from the sides of the pan and center is almost firm when tested with a toothpick (a few moist crumbs cling to the pick).

OH HENRY BARS

4 c. quick oatmeal
1 c. brown sugar
1 c. margarine
1/2 c. white Karo syrup

Mix above ingredients together as you would a pie crust. Spread into 10" × 15" pan and bake in 350 oven for 10-15 minutes, until golden brown. Melt 6-oz. package chocolate chips and 3/4 c. chunky peanut butter and spread over the above.

🌲 🌲 🌲 🌲 🌲

CHOCOLATE FILLED OATMEAL BARS

3/4 c. butter
1 c. brown sugar
1/2 tsp. salt
1 1/2 c. flour
1 1/4 c. quick oatmeal
1 14-oz. can condensed milk
1 c. chocolate chips
1/2 c. nuts or coconut, chopped

Cream butter with brown sugar and salt. Blend in flour and oats. Press 2/3 c. mixture into bottom of greased 9" × 13" pan. Heat condensed milk; stir in chips and nuts. Pour over mixture in pan. Sprinkle with remaining crumbs. Bake at 350 for 30-35 minutes. Cut into bars.

PUMPKIN COOKIE BARS

1 c. flour
1/2 c. quick oats
1/2 c. brown sugar, firmly packed
1/4 c. nuts, chopped
1 3/4 tsp. cinnamon
1/2 c. butter, melted
1 c. pumpkin
3/4 c. undiluted Evaporated milk
1 egg, slightly beaten
1/3 c. sugar
1/2 tsp. allspice
1/4 tsp. salt

Combine flour, oats, brown sugar, nuts and 1 tsp. cinnamon. Add butter; mix until crumbly. Press into bottom of 13" × 9" × 2" pan. Bake at 350 for 12-15 minutes. Reduce temperature to 325. Combine remaining ingredients. Pour over crust. Bake at 325 for 25-30 minutes or until toothpick inserted in center comes out clean. Cool completely.

Cream Cheese Topping:
1 8-oz. package cream cheese, softened
1/4 c. orange marmalade.

Beat together until fluffy.
Spread over cooled bars. Garnish with crushed granola, chopped nuts or orange peel. Cut into 32 bars.

🌲 🌲 🌲 🌲 🌲

EASY BROWNIES

2 c. sugar
1 c. flour
6 Tbsp. cocoa
2 sticks butter (melted with cocoa)
4 eggs
2 tsp. vanilla
1/2 c. pecans

Mix and pour all ingredients over cocoa and butter. Mix by hand—DO NOT over mix. Grease and flour 9" × 13" pan. Bake at 325 for 30-35 minutes. Let set before cutting.

CHOCOLATE PEPPERMINT BARS II

Layer 1:
>2 oz. unsweetened chocolate
>1/2 c. butter
>2 eggs
>1 c. sugar
>1/2 c. flour, sifted
>1/2 c. chopped almonds (optional)

Melt chocolate and butter. Cream eggs and sugar. Add flour and chocolate mixture. Mix well. Bake in an 8" x 8" pan at 350 for 20 minutes, then turn oven off and bake 5 more minutes.

Layer 2:
>1 1/2 c. powdered sugar
>3 Tbsp. butter or margarine
>2-3 Tbsp. cream
>1 tsp. peppermint extract, tinted red or green

Cream sugar and butter. Blend in cream and peppermint. Spread onto cooled first layer. Refrigerate until chilled.

Layer 3:
>3 oz. unsweetened chocolate
>3 Tbsp. butter

Melt chocolate and butter together and pour over peppermint layer. Chill. Cut into small squares. Makes 20-30 bars.

🌲   🌲   🌲   🌲   🌲

SOUTHERN PINEAPPLE BAR COOKIES

>1 can (20 oz.) crushed pineapple
>1 c. flour
>1/3 c. butter or margarine, melted
>1/2 c. sliced almonds
>1/2 c. sugar
>1 8-oz. package cream cheese, softened
>1 egg
>1 tsp. vanilla extract
>1/3 c. flaked coconut

Drain pineapple. Mix flour and butter. Chop 1/4 c. almonds; add to mixture with 1/4 c. sugar. Mix until crumbly. Press into 9" square pan. Bake at 350 for 12 minutes. Beat cream cheese, egg, remaining 1/4 c. sugar, vanilla and pineapple. Pour over crust. Top with coconut and remaining 1/4 c. sliced almonds. Continue to bake 35-40 minutes until golden brown. Cool on wire rack. Refrigerate at least 2 hours before cutting into bars. Makes 16 bars.

PINEAPPLE BARS

Mix and press into 9" × 9" pan. Bake at 350 for 15 minutes.
    1/2 c. butter
    1/4 c. sugar
    1 1/4 c. flour
Pour over crust.
    1 c. well-drained crushed pineapple
Mix together:
    1 egg, well beaten
    1 Tbsp. butter, softened
    1/2 c. sugar
    1 1/2 c. coconut.
Spread over pineapple. Bake 20 minutes at 350. Cool. Frost with powdered sugar frosting.

PECAN DREAMS

Layer 1:
    1/2 c. butter
    1/4 c. confectioners' sugar
Combine butter, sugar and flour in mixing bowl. Mix until thoroughly blended. Pat mixture into bottom of 13" × 9" × 2" ungreased pan.

Layer 2:
    2 eggs
    2 Tbsp. flour
    1/2 tsp. baking powder
    1 c. minus 2 T. flour
    1 1/2 c. brown sugar, firmly packed
    1 c. pecans, coarsely chopped
Beat eggs lightly in small bowl. Sift together flour and baking powder. Add flour mixture and brown sugar to eggs. Mix until smooth. Stir in pecans. Spread over first layer. Bake at 375 for 30-40 minutes until golden brown. Cool. Cut into squares.

CHEESECAKE BARS

5 Tbsp. butter
1/3 c. brown sugar
1 c. flour
1/2 c. nuts, chopped
1/2 c. sugar
8 oz. cream cheese
1 egg
2 Tbsp. milk
1 Tbsp. lemon juice
1/2 tsp. vanilla

Cream butter and brown sugar. Add flour and nuts; mix. Save 1 c. of mixture for topping. Press remainder into 8" x 8" pan. Bake at 350 for 12-15 minutes. Blend sugar and cream cheese until smooth. Add egg, milk, lemon juice and vanilla. Beat well. Spread over bottom crust. Sprinkle with reserved 1 c. topping. Return to 350 oven and bake 25 minutes. Cool. Chill and cut into bars. May double and bake in 9" x 13" pan.

🌲 🌲 🌲 🌲 🌲

PEANUT BUTTER BROWNIES

1 c. peanut butter
1/2 cube butter
1 1/2 c. plus 1 Tbsp. sugar
1 c. flour
3-4 Tbsp. cocoa
4 eggs
1/2 tsp. vanilla
1/3 tsp. salt

Mix and spread into greased pan. Bake at 350 for 20-30 minutes. When slightly cool, sprinkle with powdered sugar.

ROCKY MOUNTAIN BARS

Brownie-like texture with rocky road candy flavor. These are delicious!!

Crust:
- 1/2 c. butter
- 1 oz. unsweetened chocolate
- 1 c. flour
- 1 tsp. baking powder
- 2 large eggs
- 1 c. sugar
- 1 tsp. pure vanilla extract
- 1/2 c. nuts, chopped

Melt butter and chocolate; cool. Sift together flour and baking powder. In medium bowl, beat eggs, sugar and vanilla. Add chocolate mixture to eggs, beating well. Add flour mixture and nuts. Spread into buttered 9" x 13" pan. Set aside.

Filling:
- 6 oz. cream cheese, softened
- 4 Tbsp. butter, softened
- 1/2 c. sugar
- 1 large egg
- 1/2 tsp. pure vanilla extract
- 2 Tbsp. flour
- 1/4 c. nuts, chopped
- 6 oz. semi-sweet chocolate chips
- 2 c. miniature marshmallows

Beat together cream cheese, butter and sugar until fluffy. Add egg, vanilla and flour. Beat well. Stir in nuts and spread batter over unbaked crust. Sprinkle with chocolate chips. Bake at 350 for 30-35 minutes. Remove from oven and sprinkle with marshmallows. Return to oven for 2 minutes.

Frosting:
- 4 Tbsp. butter
- 1 oz. unsweetened chocolate
- 2 oz. cream cheese
- 1/4 c. whole milk
- 1 tsp. pure vanilla extract
- 3 c. powdered sugar

Melt together butter and chocolate; cool. Add cream cheese, milk, vanilla and powdered sugar; beat until smooth. Spread over marshmallow layer. Cool and cut into bars. Makes 24 bars.

GREAT AMERICAN
CHOCOLATE CHIP COOKIES

1 c. butter, softened
3/4 c. sugar
3/4 c. light brown sugar, packed
1 tsp. vanilla
2 eggs
2 1/4 c. flour
1 tsp. soda
1/2 tsp. salt
2 c. chocolate chips
1 c. chopped nuts (optional)

Mix well and spread into greased jelly roll pan. Bake at 375 for 20 minutes. Cut into squares.

🌲 🌲 🌲 🌲 🌲

PECAN PIE BARS

2 c. flour, unsifted
1/2 c. confectioners' sugar
1 c. cold margarine or butter
1 14-oz. can sweetened condensed milk
1 egg
1 tsp. vanilla
1 6-oz. package almond brickle chips
1 c. pecans, chopped

Preheat oven to 350 (325 for glass dish). In medium bowl, combine flour and sugar; cut in margarine until crumbly. Press firmly onto bottom of 13" x 9" baking pan. Bake 15 minutes.

Meanwhile, in medium bowl, beat sweetened condensed milk, egg and vanilla. Stir in chips and pecans. Spread evenly over crust. Bake 25 minutes or until golden brown. Cool. Cut into bars. Store covered in refrigerator.

LEMON BUTTER BARS

2 c. all-purpose flour, unsifted
1 c. unsalted butter, softened
1/2 c. plus 1 Tbsp. confectioners' sugar
4 eggs
2 c. granulated sugar
1 tsp. baking powder
1/2 tsp. salt
2/3 c. lemon juice, freshly squeezed

Preheat oven to 350. Beat together flour, butter and the 1/2 c. confectioners' sugar, in a small bowl with electric mixer, until well blended. Press into bottom of 13" × 9" pan. Bake 25-30 minutes or until lightly golden. Beat eggs, granulated sugar, baking powder, salt and lemon juice in small bowl until smooth.. Pour over hot crust. Bake 15 minutes more or until bubbly and lightly browned. Cool completely in pan on wire rack. Dust lightly with remaining confectioners' sugar. Cut into diamond shapes about 2 1/2" × 1 1/2". Use small spatula to lift the diamonds out of pan to store in an airtight container at room temperature.

🌲 🌲 🌲 🌲 🌲

RASPBERRY DIAMOND COOKIES

"These melt in your mouth"

1 c. butter, softened
3 Tbsp. sugar
2 c. flour
1 12-oz. jar raspberry preserves
1 recipe Vanilla Butter Cream Frosting

Cream butter and sugar. Add flour. Pat dough into 10" × 15" × 1" baking sheet. Bake at 375 for 15 minutes. Do not brown.
When cool, slice into diamond shapes by making diagonal cuts on cookie 1 1/2" apart. Decorate each cookie with a strip of raspberry preserves and a strip of vanilla butter cream frosting on either side of the preserves. Makes 2 dozen.

Butter cream frosting:
2 Tbsp. butter
3 Tbsp. milk
2-2 1/2 c. powdered sugar (use more if not stiff enough)
1 tsp. vanilla

Beat together until smooth.

Drop Cookies

PECAN CRUNCH COOKIES

1 c. butter, softened
6 Tbsp. powdered sugar
2 c. flour, unsifted
2 c. pecan meats, cut larger than ordinary
1 dessert spoon vanilla
1 Tbsp. water

Mix like pie dough. Drop by teaspoonfuls onto a baking sheet. Bake at 275 for 45 min. Roll in powdered sugar.

FORGOTTEN KISSES

2 egg whites
pinch of salt
pinch of cream of tarter
2/3 c. sugar
1 package chocolate mint chips (or regular chips and mint extract)
Green food coloring (or red)

Heat oven to 350. Beat whites until frothy. Add salt and tartar. Keep beating, gradually adding sugar. Fold in food coloring and chips. Drop onto ungreased baking sheets. Turn oven off and leave cookies in oven several hours or over night. Makes about 24 cookies.
Variations:

FOR SANTA'S KISSES:
Preheat oven to 350. Beat 2 egg whites; while beating gradually add 1/4 tsp. cream of tarter and 1/2 c. sugar. When stiff, add 1/3 tsp. salt and 1/2 tsp. vanilla. Fold in 3 1/4-oz. can flaked coconut. Drop onto brown paper on a cookie sheet. Bake 20 minutes at 325. Peel off paper when cool.

For WITCHES KISSES at Halloween:
Fold in melted 6-oz. package chocolate chips with coconut. Can be decorated with candy corn or other Halloween candy.

CHOCOLATE CAKE COOKIES

1/2 c. butter
1 1/2 c. sugar
2 eggs
1 c. sour cream
2 3/4 c. flour
2 squares unsweetened chocolate, melted and cooled
1 tsp. vanilla
1/2 tsp. soda
1/2 tsp. baking powder
1/2 c. walnuts, chopped
1/2 tsp. salt

Cream butter and sugar; add eggs, sour cream and vanilla. Pour melted, cooled chocolate into mixture and mix well. Add dry ingredients and mix well. Drop by teaspoonfuls onto greased cookie sheet.
Bake at 350 for 10-12 minutes. They might not look done, but they are supposed to look cake-like.
Frost with:
    2 squares unsweetened chocolate
    2 Tbsp. butter
Melt the chocolate and butter together. Add 2 to 3 cups confectioners' sugar and enough milk to make a thin frosting. Dip tops of cooled cookies into frosting.

CRANBERRY DROPS

1/2 c. butter
1 c. sugar
3/4 c. brown sugar, packed
2 Tbsp. orange juice
1/4 c. milk
1 egg
3 c. flour
1 tsp. baking powder
1/4 tsp. soda
1/2 tsp. salt
1 c. nuts, chopped
2 1/2 c. cranberries, coarsely chopped

Cream butter and sugars. Beat in milk, orange juice and egg. Sift together dry ingredients. Blend well with sugar mixture. Stir in chopped nuts and cranberries. Drop by teaspoonfuls onto greased baking sheet. Bake at 375 for 10-15 minutes. Note: DO NOT store in air tight container.

AUNT NORMA'S CHRISTMAS CUPCAKES

1 c. sugar
2/3 c. butter
2 eggs
1 tsp. cinnamon
1 tsp. cloves
1 tsp. soda in 1 c. boiling water
1 lb. walnuts
1 lb. dates, chopped
1 lb. raisins or currants

Mix butter and sugar. Add eggs and soda water. Add remaining ingredients. Bake at 400 for 15 minutes in tiny cupcake papers. Makes 5-6 dozen.

JINGLE BELL COOKIES

1 lb. butter
1 1/2 c. brown sugar, packed
2 eggs
3 1/2 c. flour
4 slices green candied pineapple, cut up
1/2 lb. candied cherries, red and green
1 1/2 lb. dates, cut up
1 c. whole filberts
1 c. pecans, broken
1 c. walnuts, broken
1 tsp. soda
1 tsp. vanilla
Dash of salt

Combine and mix all ingredients. Drop onto ungreased baking sheet. Bake at 350 for 10 minutes. Don't overbake. Makes 4 dozen.

GLAZED, FLOURLESS OATMEAL LACE WAFERS

Preheat oven to 350.
Beat:
   3 whole eggs
Add gradually, beating constantly:
   2 c. sugar
Stir in:
   2 Tbsp. butter, melted
   3/4 tsp. vanilla
   1 tsp. salt
   2 c. sugar
   1 c. shredded coconut
   2 c. uncooked rolled oats
Line cookie sheet with foil. Drop the dough by half teaspoonfuls 1" apart. Bake about 10 minutes or until the edges are lightly browned. Lift foil from pan; cool until wafers can easily be removed. Makes 5 dozen.

🌲 🌲 🌲 🌲 🌲

CHOCOLATE YUMMIES

   2 c. Bisquick baking mix
   1/2 c. sugar
   1 4-oz. package chocolate pudding and pie filling
   1/2 c. flaked coconut
   1 egg
   1/3 c. milk
   2 Tbsp. butter, softened
   1 tsp. vanilla
   1 can Betty Crocker chocolate frosting
   Walnut halves
Heat oven to 350.
Mix all ingredients except frosting and walnuts.
Drop dough by 1/2 or rounded teaspoonfuls (depending on size you want) onto ungreased baking sheet.
Bake about 12 minutes.
Immediately remove from baking sheet. Cool and frost. Top each with a walnut half.
Makes 3 dozen (or 6 dozen depending on how you drop them).

CASHEW COOKIES

1/2 c. butter*
1 c. brown sugar, packed
1 egg
1/2 tsp. vanilla
2 c. sifted flour
3/4 tsp. baking powder
3/4 tsp. baking soda
1/4 tsp. salt
1/3 c. sour cream
1 c. salted cashews
1/2 tsp. cinnamon, optional
1/4 tsp. nutmeg, optional

Cream together butter and sugar. Add egg and vanilla. Sift dry ingredients together and add to creamed mixture along with sour cream. Drop onto greased cookie sheet. Bake at 350 or 400 for 6-10 minutes.
Frosting:

1/2 c. butter*
3 Tbsp. coffee cream
1/4 tsp. vanilla
2 c. powdered sugar, sifted

Brown butter; add cream and vanilla very carefully.
Mix with sugar. Frost while warm.
*This recipe must use butter.

🌲 🌲 🌲 🌲 🌲

PINEAPPLE DATE-NUT COOKIES

1 c. brown sugar, packed
1/2 c. butter or margarine
1 c. crushed pineapple, drained
2 c. flour
1/4 tsp. soda
1 tsp. baking powder
1/4 tsp. salt
1 tsp. vanilla
1 c. nuts, chopped
1/2 c. dates, chopped

Cream brown sugar and shortening together. Combine flour, soda, baking powder and salt. Mix the above together with the drained pineapple and vanilla. Add the nuts and dates. Drop by teaspoonfuls onto ungreased cookie sheet. Bake 15 minutes at 350. Cool and frost with butter icing. Makes about 3 dozen.

AMISH SUGAR COOKIES

4 1/2 c. flour, sifted
1 tsp. baking soda
1 tsp. cream of tartar
1 c. butter or margarine
1 c. cooking oil
1 c. sugar
1 c. confectioners' sugar, sifted
2 eggs
1 tsp. vanilla
1 c. walnuts, chopped
sugar

Sift together flour, baking soda and cream of tartar; set aside. Cream together butter, oil, 1 c. sugar and confectioners' sugar in mixing bowl until light and fluffy, using electric mixer at medium speed. Add eggs, one at a time, beating well after each addition. Blend in vanilla.

Gradually stir dry ingredients into creamed mixture, mixing well. Add walnuts. Drop mixture by rounded teaspoonfuls, about 3 inches apart, on greased baking sheets. Flatten each with bottom of drinking glass dipped in sugar. Bake in 375 oven for 10 minutes, or until lightly browned around the edges. Remove from baking sheets. Cool on rack.

🌲 🌲 🌲 🌲 🌲

BEACON HILL COOKIES

1/8 tsp. salt
2 egg whites
1/2 c. sugar
1/2 tsp. vinegar
1/2 tsp. vanilla
1/2 c. flaked coconut
1/4 c. walnuts, chopped
1 c. chocolate chips, melted

Add salt to egg whites and beat until foamy throughout. Add sugar gradually, beating well after each addition. Continue beating until stiff peaks form. Add vinegar and vanilla and beat well. Fold in chocolate, nuts and coconut.

Drop by teaspoonfuls onto greased baking sheet. Bake in 350 oven for 10 minutes. Makes 2 1/2 -3 dozen cookies.

GUMDROP DROPS

1/2 c. shortening
1/2 c. granulated sugar
1/2 c. brown sugar
1 egg
1 tsp. vanilla
1 c. flour
1/2 tsp. baking powder
1/2 tsp. salt
3/4 c. quick cooking oats, uncooked
1/2 c. fruit flavored gum drops, chopped
1/2 c. coconut, optional

Cream shortening and sugars. Beat in egg and vanilla until light and fluffy. Add flour, baking powder and salt. Mix well. Stir in oats, gumdrops and coconut. Drop batter by rounded teaspoonfuls onto greased cookie sheets. Bake at 350 for 12-14 minutes. Makes 3 1/2 dozen. 65 calories each.

CHRISTMAS ROCK

2 c. butter
3 c. brown sugar
4 eggs, well beaten
1/2 c. cream
2 tsp. vanilla
2 tsp. salt
2 tsp. cinnamon
2 tsp. soda
5 c. flour
2 lb. dates
1 lb. raisins
1 lb. walnuts
1 lb. almonds
1 lb. pecans
1 1/2 lb. candied cherries
3 slices of candied pineapple

Cut up fruit and nuts. Add 2 1/2 c. flour to cut up fruit and nuts so they don't stick. Cream butter and sugar. Add eggs, cream, vanilla, salt, soda and cinnamon. Mix well. Then add remaining 2 1/2 c. flour, mix well. Add fruit, nuts and flour mixture all together. Mix well. (Mix with hands.) Grease cookie sheet and bake 10 minutes at 350. You will need a large bowl or pan to mix in. They freeze well.

PUMPKIN COOKIES

1 c. shortening
1 c. sugar
1 c. canned pumpkin
1 tsp. vanilla
1 egg
2 c. flour
1 tsp. baking powder
1 tsp. baking soda
1 tsp. cinnamon
1 tsp. salt
1 c. raisins and/or chopped nuts
Caramel icing

Cream shortening and sugar; add pumpkin, vanilla and egg. Sift dry ingredients; add to mixture. Add raisins and/or nuts.

Drop by teaspoonfuls onto cookie sheets. Bake at 350 for 10-12 minutes. Yield: 3-4 dozen.

Caramel Icing:
3 Tbsp. butter
1/2 c. brown sugar
3/4 tsp. vanilla
4 Tbsp. milk
1 c. powdered sugar, sifted

Combine butter, vanilla, milk and brown sugar. Cook, stirring constantly, to rolling boil. Cool; stir in powdered sugar. Frost cookies while warm. Return to heat if mixture becomes too thick.

Cream cheese frosting can also be used:
3 oz. cream cheese
1 Tbsp. milk
6 Tbsp. butter
2/3 c. powdered sugar
1 tsp. vanilla

Beat until smooth. Spread on cookies.

Hint

When storing more than one kind of cookie, keep them separate. Crisp cookies will absorb moisture from soft cookies and become soggy.

CHRISTMAS COOKIES

1 1/2 c. brown sugar
1/2 c. butter
4 eggs, beaten
3 Tbsp. milk in 2/3 c. bourbon
3 c. flour
1 tsp. allspice
1 tsp. cinnamon
1 tsp. nutmeg
1 lb. raisins, dark
1/2 lb. candied pineapple
1/2 lb. candied cherries
1 1/2 lb. pecans

Cream brown sugar, butter and eggs. Add milk mixture. Add remaining ingredients, adding the fruits and nuts the very last. Drop by teaspoonfuls onto greased cookie sheets. Bake at 300 for 15 minutes.

ORANGE-NUT TEA DROPS

These are rich, but not too sweet, and nice to go with coffee because they can be made small.

1/2 c. butter or margarine, softened
3-oz. package cream cheese, softened
1/2 c. sugar
1 egg
1 tsp. orange rind, grated
1 tsp. vanilla
1 c. sifted flour
1/2 tsp. salt
1/2 c. pecans and walnuts, mixed

Cream together the butter, cream cheese, sugar, egg, orange rind and vanilla. Mix in flour and salt which have been sifted together. Stir in nuts. Drop by teaspoonfuls 1" apart onto lightly greased baking sheet. Bake at 350 for about 15 minutes or until just delicately brown.

BROWNIE DROPS

2 bars German Sweet Chocolate
1 Tbsp. butter
2 eggs
3/4 c. sugar
1/4 c. flour, unsifted
1/4 tsp. baking powder
1/4 tsp. cinnamon, optional
1/8 tsp. salt
1/2 tsp. vanilla
3/4 c. pecans, chopped

Melt chocolate and butter over hot water (or in the microwave). Stir and cool. Beat eggs until foamy, then add sugar, 2 Tbsp. at a time. Beat until thickened (5 minutes with electric mixer). Blend in chocolate. Add flour, baking powder, salt and cinnamon; blend. Stir in vanilla and nuts.
Drop by teaspoonfuls onto greased baking sheet. Bake at 350 for 10-12 minutes; cookie feels set when lightly touched. Makes about 36 cookies.

COCONUT SNOWBALLS

2 1/2 c. flour
1/2 tsp. soda
1/4 tsp. salt
3/4 c. butter or margarine
1 c. sugar
2 eggs
1 c. flaked coconut
3/4 c. orange juice (fresh or frozen)

Sift, then measure flour. Sift three times with salt and soda. Cream butter and sugar well. Add the beaten eggs. Alternate dry ingredients with orange juice. Drop onto cookie sheet and bake at 350 for 8-10 minutes. Frost with powdered sugar icing using orange juice for liquid instead of cream. A little coconut may be sprinkled on top, if desired.

NUTRA-PUMPKIN COOKIES

1 1/2 c. raw or brown sugar
1/2 c. shortening
1 c. pumpkin
1 egg
1 tsp. vanilla
1 tsp. nutmeg
1 tsp. cinnamon
1 tsp. salt
1 tsp. baking powder
1 tsp. baking soda
2 1/2 c. whole wheat flour
1/2 c. nuts
1 c. raisins

Put sugar, shortening, pumpkin, egg and vanilla in mixer bowl and blend. Add spices, salt, baking powder, soda and flour. Blend again. Add nuts and raisins. Blend only enough to mix thoroughly. Drop by teaspoonfuls onto greased baking sheets. Bake at 400 for 10-12 minutes. Yield: 4 dozen.

🌲　🌲　🌲　🌲　🌲

POTATO CHIP COOKIES

Surprisingly like shortbread!

1 lb. butter (or half butter & half margarine)
1 c. sugar
1 tsp. vanilla
3 1/2 c. flour
2 c. potato chips, crushed
1/2 c. pecans, chopped

Cream butter and sugar. Add vanilla and stir in flour. Add potato chips and nuts. Drop by teaspoonfuls onto greased cookie sheet. May put fairly close together as they do not spread. Bake at 350 for 15 minutes. Good keepers.

JUMBO COOKIES

1 c. boiling water
2 c. dark seedless raisins
4 c. all-purpose flour, sifted
1 tsp. baking powder
2 tsp. salt
2 tsp. ground cinnamon
1/2 tsp. ground allspice
1/2 tsp. ground nutmeg
1 tsp. baking soda
1 tsp. ground ginger
1 tsp. ground cloves
1 c. butter
1 c. sugar
1 c. brown sugar
3 eggs, slightly beaten
1 tsp. vanilla
1 c. nuts, chopped

Preheat oven to 350. Grease cookie sheets.
Add boiling water to raisins in saucepan; allow to boil 5 minutes. Remove from heat to cool. Sift together flour, baking powder, baking soda, salt, cinnamon, allspice, nutmeg, ginger and cloves. Work butter in a bowl until creamy. Add sugars and beat until well blended. Add eggs and vanilla and beat well. Gradually add sifted dry ingredients, beating well after each addition. Mix in cooled raisins and nuts. Drop slightly rounded teaspoonfuls of dough 2" apart onto prepared sheets. Bake at 350 for 10-12 minutes. Store in sealed container for 2-3 days before serving. Makes 10 dozen.

🌲 🌲 🌲 🌲 🌲

ANISE SNOW CAPS

6 eggs
3 c. all-purpose flour
1 16-oz. package powdered sugar
4 tsp. anise seed

Grease 4 large cookie sheets. In large mixer bowl, beat eggs well. Add powdered sugar. Continue beating 10 minutes. Gradually add flour and anise seed. Drop by 1/2 teaspoonfuls onto cookie sheets, allowing room for spreading. Let stand at room temperature overnight. The top of each cookie forms a smooth cap or crust.
Preheat oven to 325. Bake 10-15 minutes. Remove from oven while still white. Makes 17-18 dozen. About 20 calories per cookie.

NUT LACE COOKIES

1/2 c. butter or margarine, softened
1/2 c. sugar
1 c. pecans or almonds, finely chopped
2 Tbsp. flour
2 Tbsp. milk

In a small sauce pan over low heat, cook and stir all ingredients only until butter melts and all is well blended. Remove from heat. Drop by level teaspoonfuls 3" apart on well greased and floured cookie sheet. Bake one sheet at a time on middle rack 5-6 minutes at 350. Place cookie sheet on a rack to cool for about a minute or until firm enough to handle.
For flat cookies: remove from rack.
For arched cookies: drape over a rolling pin.
For cylinder shaped cookies: roll up jelly roll style and cool with seam side down.
Work quickly. If cookies become too hard, return to oven 15-20 seconds to soften. Yield: 48 cookies.

MINCEMEAT HERMITS

1 c. flour, sifted
1/4 tsp. soda
1/4 tsp. salt
1/4 tsp. nutmeg
1/2 tsp. cinnamon
1/3 c. butter, softened
1/3 c. dark brown sugar, packed
1 egg
2/3 c. mincemeat
1/2 Tbsp. sour cream or buttermilk

Sift flour, soda, salt and spices together. Cream butter and sugar. Add egg and beat until light. Add dry ingredients, mincemeat and cream. Mix well. Drop by teaspoonfuls onto greased cookie sheets. Bake at 400 for 10-12 minutes. Remove to racks to cool.

BLACK FOREST COOKIES

Luscious, soft drop cookies are made with the traditional ingredients of the famous German Cake.

1 8-oz. package semi-sweet chocolate squares
1 16-oz. can pitted dark sweet cherries in light syrup
2 3/4 c. all-purpose flour
shortening
3/4 c. sugar
3/4 c. milk
1 Tbsp. lemon juice
1/2 tsp. baking soda
1/2 tsp. salt
1/2 tsp. almond extract

In heavy, small saucepan over low heat, melt 2 squares of chocolate until smooth, stirring occasionally. Remove from heat. With knife, coarsely chop 4 squares of chocolate; set aside. Drain cherries, reserving 1/4 c. cherry liquid; coarsely chop cherries. Pat cherries dry with paper towel. Preheat oven to 400. Into large bowl, measure melted chocolate, reserved cherry juice, flour, 1/2 c. shortening and remaining ingredients. With mixer at low speed, beat ingredients until blended, occasionally scraping bowl with rubber spatula. Stir in cherries and chopped chocolate.

Drop dough by level tablespoonfuls, as many as possible, about 2" apart onto cookie sheet. Bake cookies 10-12 minutes until lightly browned. Remove cookies to wire racks to cool.

When cookies are cooled, drizzle over the top a mixture of 2 squares chocolate melted with 1 tsp. shortening. Let chocolate dry about 30 minutes. Store cookies in tightly covered container . Makes about 5 dozen cookies.

Hint

For cookies kept for short periods of time, it is best to store in a tightly covered tin at room temperature. Be sure to cool completely before putting them away.

OATMEAL COOKIES

Cream together:
- 1 c. shortening
- 1 c. brown sugar
- 1 c. white sugar
- 2 eggs

Add and cream again:
- 2 c. flour
- 1 tsp. soda
- 1/2 tsp. salt
- 1 tsp. baking powder
- 2 tsp. vanilla

Mix in remaining ingredients by hand:
- 1 c. coconut
- 1 c. oatmeal
- 1 c. nuts
- 1 c. bran
- 1 c. chocolate chips or raisins

Drop by teaspoonfuls onto cookie sheet. Bake at 350 for about 12 minutes.

CORNFLAKE COOKIES

- 2 c. flour
- 1 tsp. baking soda
- 1/2 tsp. salt
- 1/2 tsp. baking powder
- 1 1/4 c. shortening
- 1 c. sugar
- 1 c. brown sugar
- 2 eggs
- 1 tsp. vanilla
- 2. c. coconut
- 2 c. corn flakes

Sift dry ingredients together; set aside. Cream shortening and sugars. Add egg and vanilla. Add dry ingredients to creamed mixture. Stir in coconut and corn flakes. Drop by spoonfuls onto greased baking sheet 1 1/2" apart. Bake at 350 for 8-10 minutes or until delicately brown.

PUMPKIN WALNUT COOKIES

1/2 c. butter
1 1/2 c. brown sugar, packed
2 large eggs
1 c. pumpkin
1 tsp. vanilla
1 tsp. grated lemon peel
1 tsp. lemon juice
2 1/2 c. flour, sifted
3 tsp. baking powder
1 tsp. salt
1 1/2 tsp. pumpkin pie spice
1/4 tsp. ginger
1 c. walnuts, coarsely chopped

Cream butter and sugar together until fluffly. Beat in eggs, one at a time. Stir in pumpkin, vanilla, lemon peel and juice. Resift flour with baking powder, salt and spices. Blend with butter mixture. Stir in walnuts. Drop by tablespoonfuls onto baking sheet. Bake at 375 for 12-14 minutes. Makes 2 1/2 dozen.

🌲 🌲 🌲 🌲 🌲

WALNUT SPONGE DROPS

2 eggs, separated
few grains salt
1/4 c. evaporated milk
2 c. confectioners' sugar
3 c. walnuts, finely chopped
1/2 tsp. vanilla

Beat egg yolks until thick and lemon colored; add salt and milk; blend well. Beat in the sugar a little at a time. Stir in the ground nuts, then fold in the stiffly beaten egg whites; add vanilla. The mixture should be very stiff. Drop by teaspoonfuls 2 or 3 inches apart onto a baking sheet covered with unglazed paper. Bake at 325 for 8-10 minutes.

Remove paper and cookies from the baking sheet at once. Cool before pulling cookies from paper.

Makes 5 dozen 3-inch cookies.

DOUBLE CHOCOLATE CHERRY COOKIES

1 1/4 c. margarine or butter
1 3/4 c. sugar
2 eggs
1 Tbsp. vanilla
3 1/2 c. flour
3/4 c. cocoa
1/2 tsp. soda
1/4 tsp. salt
1 1/2 10-oz. jars maraschino cherries, well drained
1 c. chocolate mini-chips
1 14-oz. can sweetened condensed milk

Preheat oven to 350. In large mixer bowl, beat margarine and sugar until fluffy. Add eggs and vanilla. Mix Well. Stir together dry ingredients. Stir into margarine mixture (dough will be stiff). Drop 1" drops onto cookie sheet about 1" apart. Press a cherry half into center of each cookie. Bake 8-10 minutes. Cool. In heavy saucepan, combine chips and sweetened milk. Over medium heat, cook and stir until chips melt. Continue to cook and stir about 3 minutes or until mixture thickens. Frost each cookie, leaving top of cherry showing. Store loosely covered at room temperature.

🌲 🌲 🌲 🌲 🌲

RAGGEDY ANN COOKIES

Cream:
    1 c. white sugar
    3/4 c. brown sugar
    1 c. cooking oil
    2 eggs
Mix together:
    2 c. corn flakes
    1/2 c. rolled oats
    1 c. coconut
    1 tsp. baking soda
    1/2 tsp. salt
    2 c. flour

Add dry ingredients to creamed mixture. Drop large spoonfuls onto ungreased cookie sheet. Bake 10-12 minutes at 325. Makes 2-3 dozen cookies.

MACARONS — From France

1 1/2 c. almonds, ground
2 1/2 c. confectioners' sugar, divided
4 egg whites

Preheat oven to 375. Line 2 cookie sheets with parchment paper. Into small bowl sift almonds and 1 1/4 c. sugar; set aside. In large mixer bowl beat egg whites until soft peaks form. Gradually beat in remaining 1 1/4 c. sugar. Continue beating until very stiff—about 5 minutes. Sift almond-sugar over meringue, fold in gently. Drop by teaspoonfuls onto cookie sheet. Bake 15 minutes. Transfer cookie, still on paper, to damp towel until cookies can be peeled easily-about 10 minutes. Makes about 4 1/2 dozen cookies. About 40 calories each.

🌲　🌲　🌲　🌲　🌲

ROCKY ROAD COOKIES

1 6-oz. package semi-sweet chocolate morsels
1/2 c. butter or margarine
2 eggs
1 c. sugar
1 1/2 c. flour—if using self-rising flour,
    omit baking powder and salt
1/2 tsp. baking powder
1/4 tsp. salt
1/2 tsp. vanilla
1 c. nuts, chopped
Approximately 4 dozen miniature marshmallows

Melt 1/2 c. of the chocolate morsels and the butter over low heat; cool. Heat oven to 400. Mix remaining chocolate morsels, eggs, sugar, baking powder, flour, salt, vanilla, nuts and chocolate mixture. Drop dough by rounded teaspoonfuls 2" apart onto ungreased baking sheet. Press a marshmallow into center of each. Bake 8 minutes or until almost no imprint remains when touched with finger. Immediately remove from baking sheet. Makes about 4 dozen cookies.

MOCHA FROSTED DROPS

1/2 c. shortening
2 1-oz. squares unsweetened chocolate
1 c. brown sugar
1 egg
1 tsp. vanilla
1/2 c. buttermilk or sour milk
1 1/2 c. all-purpose flour, sifted
1/2 tsp. baking powder
1/2 tsp. soda
1/4 tsp. salt
1/2 c. walnuts, chopped
1 6-oz. package semi-sweet chocolate pieces

Melt shortening and unsweetened chocolate together in a saucepan. Cool 10 minutes. Stir in brown sugar. Beat in the egg, vanilla and buttermilk or sour milk. Sift together dry ingredients and add to chocolate mixture. Stir in nuts and chocolate pieces. Drop from teaspoon onto greased cookie sheet. Bake at 375 for about 10 minutes. Remove from pan and cool. Frost with Mocha Frosting. Makes about 3 1/2 dozen.

Mocha Frosting:
1/4 c. butter
2 Tbsp. cocoa (regular type, dry)
2 Tbsp. instant coffee powder
dash of salt
2 1/2 c. confectioner's sugar, sifted
1 1/2 tsp. vanilla
About 3 Tbsp. milk

Cream together butter, cocoa, coffee and salt. Beat in confectioners' sugar, vanilla and milk (enough for spreading consistency).

APPLE COOKIES

1/2 c. butter or margarine
1 1/3 c. brown sugar, packed
1 egg
1/4 c. milk
2 1/4 c. flour
1 tsp. baking soda
1 tsp. cinnamon
1/2 tsp. salt
1/2 tsp. nutmeg
1 c. walnuts, chopped
1 medium apple with peel, chopped
1 c. raisins

In large mixer bowl beat butter and brown sugar until fluffy. Add egg and milk. Sift all the dry ingredients together. Slowly add to butter mixture, beating until mixed. Stir in nuts, apple and raisins. Drop dough by rounded teaspoonfuls about 2" apart onto ungreased cookie sheet. Bake at 375 for 10-12 minutes. Makes about 42 cookies.

HOLIDAY FRUIT DROPS

1 c. shortening
2 c. brown sugar, packed
2 eggs
1/2 c. buttermilk or water
3 1/2 c. all-purpose flour
1 tsp. soda
1 tsp. salt
1 1/2 c. broken pecans
2 c. candied cherries, halved
2 c. dates, cut up

Mix shortening, sugar and eggs well. Stir in buttermilk. Blend dry ingredients; stir into sugar mixture. Stir in pecans, cherries and dates. Chill at least 1 hour. Heat oven to 400. Drop rounded teaspoonfuls of dough about 2" apart on lightly greased baking sheet. Place a pecan half on each cookie. Bake 8-10 minutes until almost no imprint remains. Makes about 8 dozen.

OATMEAL COOKIES "THE BEST"

Note: Delicious Secret is soaking of raisins

3 eggs, well beaten
1 c. raisins
1 tsp. vanilla
1 c. butter
1 c. brown sugar
1 c. white sugar
3/4 c. pecans, chopped
2 1/2 c. flour
1 tsp. salt
1 tsp. ground cinnamon
2 tsp. baking soda
2 c. oatmeal OR 1 1/2 c. oatmeal and 1/2 c. wheat germ

Combine eggs, raisins and vanilla and let stand for 1 hour, covered with plastic wrap. Cream together butter and sugars. Add flour, salt, cinnamon and soda to sugar mixture. Mix well. Blend in egg-raisin mixture, oatmeal, wheat germ and chopped nuts. Dough will be stiff. Drop by heaping teaspoonfuls onto ungreased cookie sheet or roll in small balls and flatten slightly on cookie sheet. Bake at 350 for 10-12 or until lightly browned. Makes about 6 dozen.

CHOCOLATE AMARETTO COOKIES

1/2 c. butter or margarine, softened
3/4 c. brown sugar, firmly packed
1 large egg
2 tsp. almond extract
2 1/2 c. flour
1 1/2 tsp. baking powder
1 c. ground almonds
1/4 c. unsweetened cocoa
1/4 tsp. salt
almond slices

Heat oven to 350. In large bowl with mixer at medium speed, beat butter, sugar, egg and almond extract until fluffy. Gradually add flour, baking powder and salt at low speed. Add ground almonds and cocoa powder. Drop onto ungreased cookie sheet 1 1/2" apart. Press almond slice in middle of cookie. Bake 10-12 minutes until lightly browned. Cool on wire rack. Makes about 6 dozen.

LEMON DROPS

1 c. shortening
1 c. sugar
2 eggs
3 c. flour
1 tsp. baking soda
1/2 tsp. salt
1 6-oz. can concentrated lemonade, thawed

Cream shortening and sugar. Thoroughly beat in eggs. Sift flour, soda and salt. Add alternately with 1/2 of lemonade. Drop by teaspoonfuls onto a greased cookie sheet. Bake at 375 for 15 minutes. Before removing from cookie sheet, brush tops with reserved 3 oz. of lemonade. Sprinkle with sugar. Good with ice cream.

🌲　🌲　🌲　🌲　🌲

GOOD AND DELICIOUS COOKIES

1 c. brown sugar
1 c. granulated sugar
1 c. margarine
1 c. oil
1 egg
3 tsp. vanilla
1 tsp. salt
1 tsp. soda
1 tsp. cream of tarter
1 c. rolled oats
1 c. coconut
3 1/2 c. flour
1 c. rice krispies cereal
1 12-oz package chocolate chips

Mix by order of ingredients. Drop by teaspoonfuls onto baking sheet. Bake at 350 for 12-15 minutes. Makes 6 dozen cookies.

ORANGE COOKIES

3/4 c. shortening
1 1/4 c. granulated sugar
2 eggs, well beaten
3 c. all-purpose flour, sifted
2 1/4 tsp. baking powder
1 tsp. baking soda
1/2 tsp. salt
1 c. milk
1/2 c. orange juice
1 Tbsp. grated orange peel
1 tsp. vanilla

1. Cream shortening with sugar until light and fluffy.
2. Beat in eggs.
3. Sift flour once before measuring. Mix and sift flour, baking soda, baking powder and salt together. Add dry ingredients alternately with milk, mixing thoroughly after each addition.
4. Add orange juice, grated orange rind and vanilla. Mix very well.
5. Drop by teaspoonfuls onto greased cookie sheet.
6. Bake at 350 for 10-12 minutes. Cool and frost.

Yield: 5-6 dozen.

Frosting:
2 3-oz. packages cream cheese, softened
2 Tbsp. evaporated milk, undiluted
4 3/4 cups confectioners' sugar, sifted
Dash salt
1 tsp. vanilla extract

Beat until smooth. (For orange frosting: substitute orange juice for milk and grated orange rind for vanilla.)

PISTACHIO COOKIES

1 cube butter
1/2 c. sugar
2 eggs

Cream together butter and sugar. Beat in eggs.

1/2 tsp. soda
1/2 tsp. salt
1 1/2 c. flour
1 package instant pistachio pudding mix

Add and mix well.

Bake at 350 for 10-12 minutes. Any instant pudding mix can be substituted.

▲ ▲ ▲ ▲ ▲

WHITE CHOCOLATE-MACADAMIA NUT COOKIES

2 1/4 c. flour
1 tsp. soda
1 tsp. salt
1 1/2 c. sugar
1 c. butter
2 eggs
1 tsp. vanilla
12-16 oz. white chocolate chips or broken pieces of white chocolate bark
1 c. macadamia nut pieces
    (more if you feel you can float a loan at your bank)

Cream the sugar and butter together; add the eggs and vanilla. Sift the flour, salt and soda together. Add to the creamed ingredients. Add the chocolate and nuts. Drop by teaspoonfuls onto a lightly greased cookie sheet. Bake at 350 for approximately 15 minutes. Watch that they don't become overly browned. Enjoy!!

CHIQUITA HOLIDAY COOKIES

2 1/4 c. flour
2 1/2 tsp. baking powder
1/2 tsp. salt
2/3 c. shortening
1 c. sugar
2 eggs
1 tsp. vanilla
1 c. mashed bananas (2-3)

Sift together flour, baking powder and salt. Cream shortening until soft. Gradually beat in sugar until light and fluffy. Beat in eggs and vanilla. Add flour mixture alternately with mashed bananas. Blend well after each addition. Drop by tablespoonfuls onto ungreased baking sheet. Optional: sprinkle with cinnamon sugar, nuts or coconut. Bake at 375 for 12 minutes.

🌲　🌲　🌲　🌲　🌲

BUFFALO CHIPS

2 c. shortening, melted
2 c. margarine
4 c. brown sugar
4 c. white sugar
4 tsp. vanilla
8 eggs

Cream together and add:

8 c. flour
4 tsp. soda
4 tsp. baking powder
4 c. cornflakes
4 c. oatmeal
2 c. nuts, chopped
2 c. coconut
2 c. chocolate chips

Drop by spoonfuls onto slightly greased cookie sheet. Bake at 350 for 15 minutes for chewy cookies; 20 minutes for crispy cookies. MAKES TONS!!!

CHEESE SUGAR COOKIES

Cream together:
  1/2 lb. butter
  2 c. sugar
  1 tsp. vanilla
Add and mix:
  3 eggs
  1 tsp. salt
  1 lb. ricotta cheese (comes in 15-oz. tub)
Add in and mix well:
  1 tsp. baking soda
  4 c. flour
Drop by teaspoonfuls onto ungreased cookie sheet. Bake at 375 for 10 minutes. Frost with butter cream frosting.

MOLASSES CHOCOLATE CHIP COOKIES

2 c. all-purpose flour
2 tsp. pumpkin pie spice
1 tsp. baking soda
1/2 tsp. salt
1/2 c. butter at room temperature
1/2 c. dark brown sugar, packed
1 large egg
1/2 c. light molasses
3/4 c. unsweetened applesauce
1 c. walnuts, coarsely chopped
1 c. semi-sweet chocolate chips

Heat oven to 350. Lightly grease cookie sheet. Mix flour, pie spice, baking soda and salt. In large bowl, beat butter and sugar with electric mixer until fluffy. Beat in egg and molasses. With mixer on low speed, add applesauce (mixture will look curdled). Gradually add flour mixture and beat just until blended. Stir in walnuts and chocolate chips. Drop well-rounded teaspoonfuls 2" apart onto prepared cookie sheet. Bake 10 minutes or until centers of cookies feel firm when lightly touched. Cool on cookie sheet 1 minute before removing to rack to cool completely. Store tightly covered with waxed paper between layers. Makes 72.

CHRISTMAS ROOKS

2 sticks butter, softened
1 1/2 c. brown sugar, packed
2 eggs, beaten
2 1/2 c. flour, unsifted
1 tsp. cinnamon
1 tsp. soda
1 tsp. salt
1 tsp. vanilla
4 oz. candied red cherries
6 oz. candied green cherries
6 oz. candied pineapple
2 lbs. pitted dates, chopped
1 c. pecans, chopped
1 c. walnuts, chopped
2 lb. filberts, cracked, leave whole

Use large bowl. Cream butter, sugar and eggs. Mix. Reserve 3/4 c. flour. Sift together 1 3/4 c. flour, cinnamon, soda and salt. Add to creamed mixture. Add the remaining 3/4 c. flour to fruit for easier handling. Mix all and drop onto greased baking sheets. Bake at 275 for 15-20 minutes. Makes 15 dozen. Recipe may be halved.

MONSTER COOKIES

12 eggs
2 lb. brown sugar
4 c. white sugar
1 Tbsp. vanilla
1 Tbsp. white karo syrup
8 tsp. soda
1 lb. butter (no margarine)
3 lb. peanut butter
18 c. oatmeal (can use half flour)
1 lb. chocolate chips
1 lb. M & M candies

Mix in dishpan in order given. Dip by large tablespoon, ice cream scoop or 1/4 measuring cup and flatten. Place about 6 to a cookie sheet. Bake 12 minutes at 375. Do not overbake. Let cool 2-3 minutes before removing from cookie sheet.

OATMEAL DROPS

1 c. dark brown sugar, packed
1/2 c. shortening
1 egg, unbeaten
1 tsp. vanilla
Thick red jam
1/2 tsp. lemon extract
1 c. quick-cooking rolled oats
1 c. all-purpose flour, sifted
1/2 tsp. soda
1/2 tsp. salt
1/2 tsp. baking powder

Combine sugar, shortening, egg, vanilla and lemon extract in mixing bowl; beat until fluffy. Stir in oats. Sift flour with soda, salt and baking powder. Add to first mixture and mix well. Drop stiff dough by rounded teaspoonfuls onto greased baking sheets. Make a shallow "well" in center of each cookie; fill with jam. Bake at 350 about 15 minutes. Makes 3 1/2-4 dozen.

SOUR CREAM COOKIES

Measure and sift together:
   3 c. flour, sifted
   1 tsp. baking powder
   1/2 tsp. baking soda
   1 tsp. salt
   1/2 tsp. cinnamon
   1/2 tsp. nutmeg

Combine and beat well together:
   2 c. brown sugar, packed
   1 c. sour cream
   1/2 c. salad oil
   2 eggs

Add dry ingredients and stir in:
   1/2 c. chopped walnuts, optional

Drop from teaspoon onto greased cookie sheet. Moisten bottom of small glass; dip into mixture of sugar and nutmeg and flatten each cookie. Can be topped with walnut. Bake at 425 about 10 minutes.

PINEAPPLE DROP COOKIES

Cream well:
- 1 c. brown sugar
- 1/2 c. shortening
- 1 egg

Add:
- 3/4 c. drained pineapple

Sift together:
- 2 c. flour
- 1/4 tsp. salt
- 1/4 tsp. soda
- 1 tsp. baking powder

Combine flour and creamed mixture. Add 1 tsp. vanilla and 1/2 c. chopped nuts. Drop by teaspoonfuls onto greased baking sheet. Bake at 375 for 8 minutes.

Frosting:
- 1 c. powdered sugar moistened with pineapple juice. Frost cookies when cool.

OATMEAL LACE COOKIES

- 2 1/2 c. rolled oats
- 1 c. butter, melted
- 1 1/2 c. brown sugar

Mix together in bowl and let stand overnight.

Add:
- 1 egg
- 1 Tbsp. molasses
- 1 tsp. vanilla

Heat oven to 375. Drop dough by teaspoonfuls 2" apart on well greased cookie sheets. Bake 6 minutes. Remove with spatula and roll flat before cooling. Makes 6 dozen.

SPICY CARROT COOKIES

2 tsp. ground cinnamon
2 tsp. ground ginger
1 tsp. ground nutmeg
2 1/4 c. flour, unsifted
1 tsp. baking powder
1/2 tsp. baking soda
1/2 c. butter or margarine
3/4 c. dark brown sugar, firmly packed
1/4 c. sugar
1 egg
1/2 tsp. vanilla
1/2 tsp. salt
1 tsp. grated orange rind
1 1/2 c. raw carrot, finely grated
1 c. shredded coconut
1 c. walnuts, chopped
1 c. golden raisins

1. Preheat oven to 350. Grease cookie sheets.
2. Sift together dry ingredients.
3. Beat together butter, brown sugar and sugar in large bowl until well mixed. Beat in egg, vanilla and orange rind. Stir in flour mixture until well blended. Gently stir in carrot, coconut, walnuts and raisins.
4. Drop dough by teaspoonfuls onto the prepared cookie sheet, leaving about 2" between cookies.
5. Bake at 350 for 12-15 minutes or until golden brown. Remove to wire rack to cool. Store in tightly covered containers with a slice of apple or orange to keep moist.
6. Decorate with cream cheese or butter frosting and red hots if desired.

🌲 🌲 🌲 🌲 🌲

ORANGE MARMALADE DROPS

2/3 c. sugar
1/3 c. butter
1 egg
6 Tbsp. orange marmalade
1 1/2 c. flour
1 1/4 tsp. baking powder

Beat sugar and butter together until light and creamy. Beat in egg and marmalade. Sift flour and baking powder. Stir sifted ingredients into butter mixture. Drop batter by teaspoonfuls onto greased sheet. Bake at 375 for 8 minutes. (May need to adjust flour amount depending on marmalade.)

DOUBLE CHOCOLATE COOKIES

1 1/4 c. margarine
2 c. sugar
2 eggs
1 tsp. vanilla
2 c. flour, unsifted
3/4 c. cocoa
1 tsp. soda
1/2 tsp. salt
1 8-oz. package chocolate chips
1 c. nuts, chopped

Mix all ingredients together well. Drop by teaspoonfuls onto ungreased baking sheets. Bake at 350 for 8-9 minutes.

🌲 🌲 🌲 🌲 🌲

GRAND MARNIER
CHOCOLATE CHIP COOKIES

2 1/2 c. flour
2 tsp. baking powder
1/4 tsp. salt
1 c. margarine
12-oz. semi-sweet chocolate chips
1/2 c. granulated sugar
3/4 c. brown sugar
2 eggs, well beaten
1 1/2 Tbsp. Grand Marnier
1 c. walnuts, chopped
1 Tbsp. grated orange peel

Sift flour, baking powder and salt. Cream margarine and sugars until fluffy. Add eggs and blend well. Add dry ingredients to creamed mixture with Grand Marnier and orange peel. Mix and fold in chocolate chips and nuts. Drop onto ungreased baking sheets. Bake at 325 for about 20 minutes. Cool and glaze. Makes 4 dozen.

Glaze:
6-oz. semi-sweet baking chocolate
1 Tbsp. Grand Marnier
1/2 c. nuts, chopped

Dip in glaze, then in nuts.

HERMITS

3 c. brown sugar
1 c. butter
4 Tbsp. milk
4 eggs, beaten
2 tsp. soda
2 c. raisins
2 c. currants
1 c. nuts, chopped
5 c. flour
grated rind of orange
1 tsp. nutmeg
1 tsp. cinnamon

Cream butter, sugar, eggs and milk. Mix flour and soda. Add 1/2 of flour mixture to creamed mixture. Add nuts, raisins, currants, orange rind, rest of flour mixture and spices. Drop by spoonfuls onto greased cookie sheet. Makes a lot. Can be divided. Freezes well. Bake at 350 for 12-15 minutes.

🌲   🌲   🌲   🌲   🌲

CHEWY MOLASSES COOKIES

1/2 c. shortening
1 c. sugar
2 eggs
1 c. molasses
4 c. all-purpose flour
2 tsp. baking soda
1/2 tsp. salt
1 tsp. ground ginger
1 tsp. ground cinnamon
1/2 c. buttermilk

Cream shortening and sugar, beating well with mixer at medium speed. Add eggs and molasses; mix well. Combine flour and next 4 ingredients; add to creamed mixture alternately with buttermilk and ending with flour mixture. Drop dough by rounded teaspoonfuls 1 1/2" apart on lightly greased cookie sheets. Bake at 350 for 10-12 minutes. Makes 8 doz. cookies.

PISTACHIO-MINT CHOCOLATE COOKIES

1 c. butter or margarine, softened
1/2 c. vegetable shortening
1 c. granulated sugar
1/4 c. light brown sugar, firmly packed
2 large eggs
2 tsp. vanilla
3 c. all-purpose flour, unsifted
1 tsp. baking soda
1/2 tsp. salt
1 10-oz. package mint chocolate chips, or
        1 12-oz. package semi-sweet chocolate chips
1 c. shelled pistachio nuts, coarsely chopped

1. Heat oven to 375. In large bowl, with electric mixer at medium speed, beat butter, shortening, sugars, eggs and vanilla until well blended. Reduce mixer speed to low; gradually beat in flour, baking soda and salt until well mixed.
2. With wooden spoon, stir in chocolate chips and nuts. Drop dough by 1/4 cupfuls, about 3" apart, onto ungreased baking sheets.
3. Bake cookies 12-15 minutes or until lightly browned. Cool slightly on baking sheet. Remove cookies to wire rack to cool completely. Store in airtight container.

🌲 🌲 🌲 🌲 🌲

GORP COOKIES

1 c. butter, softened
1 c. brown sugar
2 tsp. milk
1 tsp. baking soda
2 c. flour
1 c. raisins
1 c. peanuts
3/4 c. chocolate chips or M & M's

Cream butter with sugar. Beat in milk and soda. Mix in flour. Stir in raisins, peanuts and chocolate chips or M & M's. Drop by teaspoonfuls onto greased baking sheets. Bake at 350 for 8-10 minutes. Cool on baking sheets for several minutes before removing from pan.

MARVELOUS CHRISTMAS MACAROONS

2 2/3 c. coconut flakes
2/3 c. sugar
1/4 c. all-purpose flour
1/4 tsp. salt
4 egg whites
1 tsp. almond extract
1 c. natural almonds, chopped
1/2 c. candied cherries

Combine coconut, flour, sugar and salt in mixing bowl. Stir in egg whites and almond extract. Stir in almonds; mix well. Drop from teaspoonfuls onto lightly greased baking sheets. Garnish with candied cherry halves. Bake at 325 for 20-25 minutes, or until edges of cookies are golden brown. Remove from baking sheets immediately. Makes about 2 1/2 dozen.

CHOCOLATE-DIPPED OATMEAL
LACE COOKIES

Simplicity itself. You just beat, drop, bake and dip.

1 large egg, beaten lightly
1/4 c. light brown sugar, firmly packed
1 c. old-fashioned rolled oats
1/4 c. granulated sugar
1/4 tsp. salt
1/4 tsp. almond extract
1 Tbsp. unsalted butter, melted and cooled
4 oz. semi-sweet chocolate, coarsely chopped

In a bowl with an electric mixer, beat the egg with the brown sugar and the granulated sugar until the mixture is thick and pale. Add the oats, salt, almond extract and butter; stir well. Drop the batter by rounded tea-spoonfuls 3" apart onto baking sheets lined with buttered foil and flatten each mound with the back of a fork dipped in water. Bake the cookies in the middle of a preheated 325 oven for 7 minutes, or until golden brown around the edges. Let the cookies cool on the baking sheets and peel them off the foil gently.

In the top of a double boiler set over barely simmering water, melt the chocolate. Holding each cookie by the edge, dip into chocolate to coat half. Put cookies on racks while the chocolate hardens. Makes about 30 cookies.

No Bake Cookies

TURTLES

2 c. pecan halves
36 pieces of unwrapped caramels
3 Tbsp. margarine
1/2 tsp. vanilla
2/3 c. semi-sweet chocolate chips
1 1/2 tsp. shortening

1. Cover baking sheet with waxed paper and arrange pecans at least 1" apart.
2. Place caramels with butter into double boiler, stirring constantly, until completely melted.
3. Remove from heat. Add vanilla. Stir.
4. Drop by teaspoonfuls onto center of each nut. Allow to cool.
5. Melt chocolate with shortening. Stir. Spread over caramel and allow to set before removing from waxed paper.

WINDOW PANE COOKIES

Melt over low heat:
    2 Tbsp. butter
    1 c. chocolate chips
Add:
    1 beaten egg
Cool. Stir in:
    3 c. miniature colored marshmallows
    1/2 c. nuts
Make into 2 long rolls; roll in coconut. Roll in waxed paper and cool in refrigerator 24 hours. Cut in slices and serve.

COCONUT JOYS

1/2 c. butter or margarine
2 c. powdered sugar
3 c. coconut
2 squares unsweetened chocolate, melted

1. Melt butter in saucepan. Remove from heat.
2. Add powdered sugar and coconut. Mix well.
3. Shape into balls.
4. Make indent in center of each and place on cookie sheet.
5. Fill centers with melted chocolate.
6. Chill until firm. Store in refrigerator. Makes 3 dozen.

SUPER COOKIES

1 c. margarine, melted
1 c. peanut butter
1 1/2 c. graham cracker crumbs
1 lb. powdered sugar
1 c. coconut

Combine and make into 1" balls. Refrigerate.
Next day, melt:

1 6-oz. package chocolate chips
1/4 bar paraffin

Dip balls and cool. Makes about 3 dozen.

STRAWBERRIES

Cook until thick:
   1/3 c. margarine
   1/2 c. sugar
   1 1/4 c. dates, cut up
Cool and add:
   pinch of salt
   1/2 tsp. vanilla
   2 c. rice krispies cereal
   1/2 nuts

Roll into strawberries. Decorate by rolling in red sugar, adding a green tissue star and inserting 1/2 of a green toothpick. For Christmas, roll balls in red and green sugar. Makes 3 dozen.

🌲 🌲 🌲 🌲 🌲

KENTUCKY COLONELS

   2 eggs, beaten
   1 c. sugar
   1/2 stick butter or margarine, melted
   1 c. dates, cut up
   1/4 tsp. salt
   1 tsp. vanilla
   2 1/2 c. rice krispies
   1 c. nuts, chopped
   2 c. coconut

Add sugar to beaten eggs gradually. Add mixture to melted butter in saucepan with dates and salt. Cook until dates are melted; add vanilla. Pour mixture over rice krispies and nuts. Mix. Drop teaspoonfuls of mixture into coconut and roll until covered. Makes 4 dozen.

OATMEAL FUDGE COOKIES

Boil 1 minute:
    2 c. sugar
    1/2 c. margarine
    6 Tbsp. cocoa
    1/2 c. milk
Remove from heat and stir in quickly:
    3 c. quick oats
    1 c. nuts
    1 tsp. vanilla
Drop by spoonfuls onto waxed paper.

🌲　🌲　🌲　🌲　🌲

MARSHMALLOW BALLS

Combine and cook until melted:
    6 1 3/4-oz. Heath bars, broken
    14-oz. can condensed milk
    1/4 c. margarine
Cool slightly. Dip 48 large marshmallows into mixture and roll in 1 c. rice krispies, coarsely crushed. Dry on waxed paper. Makes 4 dozen.

Hint

Make your own SWEETENED CONDENSED MILK - easy and a LOT cheaper!
This recipe makes about 14 oz. and can be used in any recipe calling for sweetened condensed milk. Keeps for several weeks under refrigeration.
    1 c. instant nonfat milk
    2/3 c. sugar
    1/3 c. boiling water
    3 Tbsp. melted butter or margarine
    Pinch of salt
Put in blender and process until smooth.

CREME DE MENTHE BALLS

2 1/2 c. vanilla wafers, finely crushed
1 c. powdered sugar, sifted
2 Tbsp. cocoa
1 c. nuts, finely chopped
1/4 c. light corn syrup
1/4 c. white Creme De Menthe
granulated sugar

Combine first four ingredients. Stir in corn syrup and Creme de Menthe. Add a few drops of water if necessary to form mixture into 1" balls. Roll in granulated sugar. Makes 3 1/2 dozen.

🌲 🌲 🌲 🌲 🌲

DOUBLE-CHOCOLATE CHERRY BOURBON BALLS

These sinfully delicious chocolate confections are best after several days' storage.

1 6-oz. package semi-sweet chocolate pieces
3 Tbsp. corn syrup
1/2 c. bourbon*
1 8 1/2-oz. package chocolate wafers, crushed
1 c. nuts, finely chopped
1/2 c. confectioners' sugar
1/4 c. candied red cherries, finely chopped
Granulated sugar

In top of double boiler or bowl set over hot (not boiling) water, melt chocolate. Remove from heat; stir in corn syrup and bourbon.
In large bowl, mix well the wafer crumbs, nuts, confectioners' sugar and cherries. Add chocolate mixture; stir until blended. Let stand 30 minutes. Shape into 1" balls; roll in granulated sugar. Makes 54.
*Ginger ale can be substituted for bourbon.

CHOCOLATE-PEANUT MUNCHIES

2 c. confectioners' sugar
1 1/4 c. chunky peanut butter
1/4 c. butter or margarine, softened
2 c. rice krispies
1 6-oz. package semi-sweet chocolate chips

In bowl using mixer at medium speed, cream sugar, peanut butter and butter until well mixed. Stir in cereal.

Melt chocolate pieces in top of double boiler over hot water, but not boiling. Remove from heat. Roll peanut butter mixture into 1" balls. Dip each in chocolate, covering half the ball. Refrigerate until chocolate becomes firm. Cover and store in refrigerator. Makes about 3 1/2 dozen.

CREME DE MENTHE SQUARES

1 1/4 c. butter or margarine
1/2 c. unsweetened cocoa powder
3 1/2 c. powdered sugar, sifted
1 egg, beaten
1 tsp. vanilla
2 c. graham cracker crumbs
1/3 c. green Creme de Menthe
1 1/2 c. semi-sweet chocolate pieces

For bottom layer:

In saucepan, combine 1/2 c. of the butter with cocoa powder. Heat and stir until well blended. Remove from heat. Add 1/2 c. powdered sugar, egg and vanilla. Stir in graham cracker crumbs. Mix well. Press into bottom of an ungreased 13"x9"x2" pan.

For middle layer:

Melt another 1/2 c. butter. In a small mixer bowl, combine melted butter and Creme de Menthe. At low speed, beat in remaining 3 c. powdered sugar until smooth. Spread over the chocolate layer. Chill 1 hour.

For top layer:

In small saucepan, combine remaining 1/4 c. butter and chocolate pieces. Melt and spread over green layer. Chill 1-2 hours. Cut into small squares. Store in refrigerator. Seal each piece in clear plastic, wrapped for gifts. Makes about 96 squares.

CHOCOLATE TRUFFLES

3/4 c. hazelnuts, walnuts or pecans
6 1-oz. squares semi-sweet chocolate
1 1/3 c. powdered sugar
1 egg white
2 Tbsp. Grand Marnier or rum
1/3 c. heavy cream
Chocolate sprinkles

1. Grind nuts in blender. Line bottom of 9" x 5" x 3" loaf pan with wax paper.
2. In a small sauce pan, combine chocolate and cream. Heat over low heat just until chocolate is melted. Remove from heat.
3. In medium bowl, combine nuts, sugar and egg white. With wooden spoon, stir. Add chocolate mixture and liqueur. Mix well. Turn into prepared pan. Refrigerate until firm. Shape into round balls using 1/2 tsp. for each.
4. Roll each ball in chocolate sprinkles. Freezer wrap and freeze.
5. Fill fluted bonbon cups with frozen chocolates. Let thaw before serving. Makes 60 pieces.

CHINESE CHEWS

Melt over double boiler:
　　1 6-oz. package chocolate chips
　　1 6-oz. package butterscotch chips
Add:
　　1 3-oz. can Chinese noodles
　　(You can add marshmallows, too)
Mix well and drop onto waxed paper. Let stand until firm. Makes 35 servings.

PECAN COOKIE BALLS

Boil until thick:
- 1/2 stick margarine
- 1 c. sugar
- 1 egg
- 1/2 c. dates, chopped

Add:
- 1 t. vanilla
- 2 c. rice krispies
- 1/2 c. pecans, chopped

Make into balls and roll in flaked coconut.

PEANUT BUTTER BON BONS

- 1 stick margarine
- 1 lb. powdered sugar
- 2 c. chunky peanut butter
- 2-3 c. Special K

Mix all ingredients. Roll into balls. Chill. Melt 1 12-oz. package chocolate chips and 3/4 bar paraffin. Dip balls and place on waxed paper on a cookie sheet. Freezes well. Makes 100 balls.

CHOCOLATE SCOTCHEROOS

1 c. sugar
1 c. light corn syrup
1 c. peanut butter
6 c. rice krispies

Combine sugar and syrup. Cook over moderate heat until it bubbles. Remove from heat. Stir in peanut butter. Add rice krispies. Press into greased 9" × 13" pan.

1 c. semi-sweet chocolate bits
1 c. butterscotch bits

Sprinkle over top of warm cookies. Briefly melt under oven broiler. Spread until all chunks are smooth. For best serving consistency, cool completely. Cut into squares.

COOKIE LOGS

Melt:
4 1-oz. squares semi-sweet chocolate
2 Tbsp. butter

Mix in small bowl:
1 egg
1 c. powdered sugar
1 tsp. vanilla

Add chocolate to sugar mixture. Pour mixture over 1 package colored miniature marshmallows and 1/2 c. chopped nuts. Forms 3 logs. Roll in coconut. Wrap in waxed paper and chill for 30 minutes. Slice.

CHERRY MASH BARS

2. c. sugar
2/3 c. evaporated milk
1/2 c. butter
dash of salt
15 big marshmallows
6 oz. cherry chips
6 oz. chocolate chips
1 4-oz. Hershey's bar
1/2 c. peanut butter
2 c. salted peanuts, crushed
1 tsp. vanilla

Cook first five ingredients together until the marshmallows are melted. Remove from heat, add cherry chips and stir until smooth. Pour into a buttered 9" x 13" pan. Refrigerate. Melt chocolate chips and broken-up Hershey's in top of double boiler. Add peanut butter, peanuts and vanilla. Spread over top of cooled and set cherry mixture. Store, covered, in refrigerator.

🌲 🌲 🌲 🌲 🌲

PEANUT BUTTER CHOCOLATE FUDGE PINWHEELS

1 c. peanut butter chips
1 can sweetened condensed milk
1 c. semi-sweet chocolate pieces
1 tsp. vanilla
1/2 c. chocolate sprinkles or any other coating

In medium saucepan over low heat, cook peanut butter chips with half of condensed milk, stirring occasionally, just until smooth. Remove from heat. Line a cookie sheet with foil; lightly grease a 12" x 10" area. With metal spatula spread mixture evenly to cover greased area. When slightly cooled, pat gently to even out. Let cool for 30 minutes. Repeat cooking process with chocolate bits. Stir in vanilla. Cool slightly. Spread over peanut butter layer. Let cool for 30 minutes. Lifting long side of foil gently roll both layers together jelly roll fashion. Roll log in sprinkles, pressing gently. Wrap tightly in plastic wrap. Store in cool place up to 2 weeks. Cut at room temperature.

MICROWAVE FUDGE

1 lb. confectioners' sugar
1/2 c. cocoa
1/2 c. margarine
1/4 c. plus 1 Tbsp. milk
1 tsp. vanilla
1/2 c. walnuts
1 c. miniature marshmallows

Mix all ingredients in 3 quart glass bowl. Microwave on high for 2 minutes. Stir. If marshallows are not melted, microwave 30 seconds longer. Stir until blended. Pour into 8" square buttered pan. Cover and refrigerate until set. Makes 64 pieces.

🌲 🌲 🌲 🌲 🌲

CANADIAN BARS

1/2 c. butter
4 Tbsp. cocoa
1/2 c. sugar
1 egg
2 c. graham crackers, crushed
1 Tbsp. vanilla
Vanilla pudding mix (not instant)
6 Tbsp. milk
3 1/2 c. powdered sugar
Giant Hershey chocolate bar
1/2 c. walnuts, chopped
1 c. flaked coconut

Place butter, sugar, cocoa, vanilla and egg in double boiler over hot water. Stir until soft and creamy, like custard. Combine nuts, crumbs and coconut. Add to mixture. Mix well and pack into 10" x 15" pan.

Melt 1/2 c. butter. Add 6 Tbsp. milk to which has been added 4 Tbsp. vanilla pudding mix. Cook only a few seconds, stirring constantly. Remove from heat. Stir in 3 1/2 c. powdered sugar. Spread over first part. Cool. Melt chocolate bar with a little water. Spread over top. Keep chilled.

PEANUT BUTTER BALLS

1/2 c. peanut butter
1 tsp. vanilla
2/3 c. coconut
1/4 c. nuts, chopped
1 tsp. lemon rind
1/2 c. raisins

Mix well and form into balls. Roll in some extra coconut. Chill until firm.

🌲　🌲　🌲　🌲　🌲

ORANGE JUICE SNOWBALL COOKIES

1 small box vanilla wafers
1 lb. powdered sugar
1 stick margarine, softened
1 6-oz. can frozen orange juice, thawed

Crush wafers. Add other ingredients. Chill 1/2 hour. Form into 1" balls, then roll in coconut.

Hint

The best cookies to send in the mail are bar cookies, oatmeal cookies and most moist-textured cookies. If both crisp and soft cookies are sent together, wrap them separately. Pack cookies in a sturdy container. Fill the bottom with an even layer of something like crumpled paper, plain popcorn, bubble plastic wrap or styrofoam packing material. Arrange cookies tightly together, separating layers with waxed paper or aluminum foil. Fill any spaces with packing material. Seal the package with mailing tape and ship to arrive as quickly as possible.

GRAHAM COOKIES

1 1-lb. box graham crackers
1 c. margarine
1 c. sugar
1 egg
1/2 c. milk
1 c. graham cracker crumbs
1 c. nuts, chopped
1 c. coconut

1. Cover 10" × 15" cookie sheet with whole graham crackers.
2. Combine margarine, sugar, egg and milk in saucepan. Bring to full boil, stirring occasionally. Remove from heat.
3. Add cracker crumbs, chopped nuts and coconut. Mix well and pour over graham crackers.
4. Frost with icing and cut into bars. Makes 45 bars.

Icing:
2 c. confectioners' sugar
1/2 c. margarine
1 tsp. vanilla

Cream sugar and margarine until light and fluffy. Add vanilla. If necessary add milk, 1 tsp. at at time, until at spreading consistency.

UNBAKED PEANUT BUTTER COOKIES

2 c. white sugar
1/2 c. butter
1/2 c. milk
6 tsp. cocoa
1/8 tsp. salt

Mix ingredients and bring to boil. Boil until soft ball stage. Remove from heat and stir in:

1/2 c. peanut butter
1 tsp. vanilla
3 c. oatmeal
1/2 c. coconut

Drop by teaspoonfuls onto waxed paper. Let stand until set.

PEANUT BUTTER BALLS II

Melt:

    1 1/2 cubes butter

Add:

    12-oz. box of Wheaties, crushed

    1 lb. powdered sugar

    2 c. peanut butter

Mix well and make into balls about the size of walnuts. Set aside.
Combine in double boiler:

    1 12-oz. package chocolate chips

    1 giant Hersheys chocolate bar

    1/2 bar paraffin wax

Melt and stir together then dip the peanut butter balls into the chocolate mixture; let cool on waxed paper.

CHOCOLATE SNOWBALLS

    2 c. chocolate chips

    1/2 c. sour cream

    1/4 tsp. salt

    3/4 c. powdered sugar

    2 c. vanilla wafers crumbs, finely crushed

    1/2 c. walnuts, chopped

Melt chocolate chips. Remove from heat. Add sour cream, salt, nuts and sugar. Mix with spoon. Blend in crumbs. Refrigerate until firm. Roll into balls. Roll in confectioners' sugar. Makes 3 dozen or more.

UNBAKED COOKIES

Cook until thick. Cool well, but DO NOT refrigerate:
  2 eggs
  1 c. sugar
  3/4 c. butter
Stir in:
  1 tsp. vanilla
  15 graham crackers, crushed
  2 1/2 c. small marshmallows
  4 Tbsp. coconut
  1 c. nuts
Press into 9" × 9" buttered pan and refrigerate overnight. Cut into squares and shake in bag of powdered sugar. Store in refrigerator.

NO BAKE COOKIES

  1 c. sugar
  1 c. dark Karo syrup
  1 3/4 c. crunchy peanut butter
  6 c. Special K cereal
Melt sugar and Karo syrup together, then add peanut butter. Mix in Special K. Put into 9" × 13" pan. Melt 6 oz. chocolate chips and 6 oz. butterscotch together and spread on top of cookie mixture. Put in refrigerator to cool. These freeze well.

CHOCOLATE-PECAN RUM BALLS

1 lb. shelled pecans, about 4 c., ground
1 8 1/2-oz. box chocolate wafers, crushed into fine crumbs
1/2 c. dark rum*
1 c. honey
Confectioners' sugar

Mix pecans, wafer crumbs, rum and honey in a large bowl. Chill 20 minutes. Shape well-rounded measuring teaspoonfuls into balls. Store air tight in cool place or refrigerate. Just before serving, roll in sugar. Makes 100.

*1/2 c. orange juice and 1 tsp. grated orange peel can be substituted for rum.

MINT FUDGE LOGS

1 7-oz. jar marshmallow cream
1 1/4 c. sugar
2/3 c. evaporated milk
1/2 c. butter
1 10-oz. package of mint chocolate chips
1/2 c. pistachio nuts, finely chopped

In heavy saucepan, combine marshmallow cream, sugar, milk and butter. Bring to a full rolling boil over moderate heat, stirring constantly. Remove from heat. Add mint-chocolate chips; stir until chips are melted and mixture is smooth. Transfer to bowl; cover with plastic wrap. Chill until firm enough to handle; divide in half. Roll into 8 1/2" logs. Roll in nuts. Chill until firm. Cut into 1/4" slices.

SCHAON'S FAVORITE NO BAKE BAR

2/3 c. whole milk
1 3/4 c. sugar
1 stick margarine
4 Tbsp. cocoa
3 c. quick oatmeal
1 tsp. vanilla
1 c. coconut

Bring to a boil milk, sugar, margarine and cocoa. Simmer 5 minutes on low heat. Cool slightly and add 3 c. oatmeal, vanilla and coconut. Mixture can be dropped by spoonfuls onto waxed paper or put in a 9" × 13" pan. Let stand until firm or cut into bars.

🌲　🌲　🌲　🌲　🌲

FANNY MAE FUDGE

Great for a gift; makes lots of small plates. Give it away before you eat it!!!

2 sticks margarine
4 c. sugar
1 c. milk
25 big marshmallows
12 oz. semi-sweet chocolate chips
2 bars unsweetened baking chocolate
13-oz. milk chocolate candy bar, broken
1 c. crushed walnuts, optional

Melt margarine; add sugar and stir. Add milk; stir until fairly warm and add marshmallows. Bring to slight boil and shut off. Add all the chocolate. Stir and add nuts. Put into large greased cookie sheet or 2 flat cake pans, depending on how thick you want the candy. Cool and cut into squares.

COCONUT RUM LOGS

1 12-oz. package vanilla wafers, coarsely crushed
1 1/2 c. walnuts, chopped
3 1/2 oz. flaked coconut
1 can sweetened condensed milk
2/3 c. rum
Powdered sugar

Combine vanilla wafer crumbs, nuts and coconut in large bowl. Stir in condensed milk and rum. Chill until firm - approximately 4 hours. Shape tablespoons of mixture into 1" logs. Roll in powdered sugar. Store in airtight container in refrigerator up to 1 month. Roll again in powdered sugar before serving.

MOCHA PECAN BALLS

1/2 c. butter or margarine
2 3/4 c. confectioners' sugar
1 Tbsp. instant coffee, powdered
1/4 c. boiling water
1/4 tsp. salt
2 c. Quaker oats, either quick or old-fashioned
1 6-oz. package semi-sweet chocolate pieces, chopped
1 c. pecans, finely chopped

Beat together butter and sugar until light and fluffy. Dissolve coffee powder in water. Blend coffee and salt into butter mixture. Stir in oats, chocolate pieces and 1/2 c. chopped pecans. Chill about 30 minutes; shape to form 1" balls. Roll in remaining pecans. Chill several hours or overnight. Store in refrigerator. Makes about 4 dozen balls. Can be frozen.

APRICOT COCONUT BALLS

These are nice to serve on a party luncheon plate or for a Holiday open house.

 1 1/2 c. dried apricots, ground
 2 c. moist shredded coconut
 1/2 c. pecans, ground
 1 c. sweetened condensed milk
 powdered sugar

Blend ground apricots, coconut and pecans. Stir in condensed milk. Shape into small balls. Roll in powdered sugar and a bit more coconut. Let stand in air until firm. Store in a cool place.

SNICKERS BARS

Tastes like real snickers candy bar!!

Melt together and put into 13" × 9" pan:
 1 c. chocolate chips
 1/2 c. peanut butter
 1/4 c. butterscotch chips
Boil for 5 minutes:
 1 c. sugar
 1/4 c. milk
 1/4 c. margarine
Add and spread on bottom layer:
 1 tsp. vanilla
 1/4 c. peanut butter
 1 c. marshmallow cream
1. Sprinkle 1 c. chopped peanuts on top.
2. Melt 20 caramels with 2 Tbsp. hot water and drizzle over white layer.
3. Make bottom layer again and spread on top. Should be refrigerated.

PEANUT BUTTER CUPS

1/3 lb. graham crackers, crushed
2 sticks butter or margarine, NOT MELTED
3 c. powdered sugar
1 c. peanut butter
2 c. chocolate chips
1/2 c. peanut butter

Mix together butter, powdered sugar and 1 c. peanut butter. Work in crushed crumbs and spread into 9" × 13" pan. Melt 2 c. chocolate chips and 1/2 c. peanut butter. Spread on top. Refrigerate. Cut as soon as chocolate is set but not hard. Cut into 1" × 2 1/2" bars. Can be put into mini-paper cups to resemble Reese's Cups.

FUDGE PEANUT BLOSSOMS

2 c. peanut butter chips
1 1/3 c. condensed milk
granulated sugar
9-oz. package milk chocolate kisses

Melt chips and milk in double boiler. Pour into 9" square pan. Cool for 45 minutes in refrigerator. Shape into 1" balls. Roll in sugar. Press kiss into center of each ball. Store in airtight container. **DO NOT** refrigerate. Makes about 4 dozen cookies.

Shaped Cookies

SITTING PRETTIES

1/2 c. butter or margarine
1/4 c. brown sugar, packed
1 egg, separated
1/2 tsp. vanilla
1 c. all-purpose flour
1/4 tsp. salt
Finely chopped nuts
Vanilla frosting
M & M's, plain or peanut

Blend butter and sugar in bowl; stir in egg yolk and vanilla. Sift in flour and salt; mix well. Chill 1 hour. Roll into 1" balls. Dip into slightly beaten egg white. Roll in nuts. Place 1" apart on cookie sheet. Bake in 350 oven for 5 minutes. Press thumb gently in center of each; bake 5 minutes longer. Cool. Fill with frosting and garnish with M & M's. Makes 2 dozen.

CINNAMON PILLOWS

1/2 c. butter
1/2 c. shortening
2 c. flour
5 Tbsp. sugar
dash of salt

Mix with pastry blender and roll into pencil strips. Cut into 1 1/2" bars. Bake on ungreased cookie sheet at 350 for 15-20 minutes. Roll in cinnamon-sugar mixture while warm. Makes 6 dozen.

NUTMEG LOGS

1 c. margarine, softened
1 tsp. rum extract
1 tsp. vanilla
3/4 c. sugar
1 egg
3 c. flour
1 tsp. nutmeg
Dash of salt

Cream margarine with flavorings; gradually add sugar and egg. Sift flour with nutmeg and salt. Add to margarine mixture. Roll handful of dough on cloth sprinkled with sugar. Cut into pieces. Bake at 350 on greased cookie sheet for 12-15 minutes. Cool and frost with powdered sugar frosting flavored with vanilla and nutmeg to taste. Sprinkle with nutmeg.

SHORTBREAD COOKIES

Mix thoroughly:
1 c. butter, softened
1/2 c. sugar
Stir in:
2 1/2 c. flour, sifted

Mix with hands, if needed. Roll 1/2" thick. Cut with miniature cookie cutters or into diagonal strips. Sprinkle with sugar or desired decorations. Bake on ungreased cookie sheet at 300 for 18-20 minutes.

SANTA'S WHISKERS

1 c. butter or margarine
1 c. sugar
1 Tbsp. milk
1 tsp. vanilla
2 1/2 c. all-purpose flour, sifted
3/4 c. red and green candied cherries, finely chopped
1/2 c. pecans, finely chopped
3/4 c. flaked coconut

In mixer bowl, cream together butter and sugar; blend in milk and vanilla. Stir in flour, candied cherries and nuts. Form into 2 rolls, each 2" in diameter and 8" long. Roll in coconut. Wrap and chill several hours or overnight. Slice 1/4" thick; place on ungreased cookie sheet. Bake in 375 oven for 12 minutes or until edges are golden. Makes about 5 dozen.

🌲 🌲 🌲 🌲 🌲

GOLDEN THUMBPRINTS

2/3 c. shortening
2/3 c. butter, softened
1 1/2 c. sugar
3 1/2 c. flour
2 tsp. baking powder
1 tsp. salt
2 eggs
2 tsp. vanilla
3/4 c. walnuts, finely chopped

Mix on low speed until blended, about 2 minutes. Gather dough into ball and chill. Roll into 1" balls. Dip in slightly beaten egg white and roll in nuts. Place on ungreased baking sheets. Bake in 375 oven for 15-18 minutes. Remove and quickly indent cookie centers. Fill with jelly or candied cherries. Cool on rack.

PEPPERMINT CANDY COOKIES

1 c. butter
1/2 c. powdered sugar
2 1/2 c. flour
1/2 c. nuts, chopped
1 tsp. vanilla
Filling:
1/2 c. peppermint candy, crushed
1/2 c. powdered sugar
2 Tbsp. cream cheese
1 tsp. milk

Cream butter with 1/2 c. powdered sugar. Gradually add flour, nuts and vanilla. Mix well and chill while preparing filling. Remove dough from refrigerator and shape into balls. Make a deep hole with your thumb in the center. Fill with 1/4 tsp. filling. Bake in 350 oven for 12-15 minutes until set but not brown. Makes 3 dozen.

FRENCH WAFFLE COOKIES

1 c. butter or margarine
1 c. brown sugar, packed
1 c. white sugar
3 eggs
1/2 tsp. vanilla
3 c. flour
1/2 tsp. soda
1 tsp. baking powder
1/4 tsp. salt

Mix and chill 8 hours or overnight. Form into small balls, walnut size. Bake 2 minutes in waffle iron in the middle temperature range. Batter keeps well in refrigerator for 2 weeks.

ICE CREAM THUMBPRINTS

4 c. flour
1 lb. margarine
1 pint vanilla ice cream

Mix together with hands (will get cold, but stick with it). Roll 1/8" thick. Cut with round cookie cutter. Make thumbprint. Fill with spoonfuls of red raspberry preserves. Bake at 375 for 19 minutes. Sprinkle with powdered sugar.

🌲 🌲 🌲 🌲 🌲

GERMAN SOUR CREAM TWISTS

3 1/2 c. flour
1 tsp. salt
1/2 c. shortening
1/2 c. butter or margarine
1 package active dry yeast
1/4 c. warm water
3/4 c. sour cream
1 whole egg and 2 egg yolks, well beaten
1 tsp. vanilla
1 c. sugar

Sift flour and salt into bowl. Cut in shortening and butter until crumbly. Dissolve yeast in water. Stir the yeast, sour cream, eggs and vanilla into flour mixture. Mix well with hands. Cover with a damp cloth and chill 2 hours.

Roll half of dough on sugared board into an oblong 8" × 16". Fold ends toward center, ends overlapping. Sprinkle with sugar. Roll again to same size and repeat a third time. Roll about 1/4" thick. Cut into strips 1" × 4". Twist ends in opposite directions, stretching dough slightly.. Put in shape of horseshoe or wreath on baking sheet. Bake 10 minutes at 350. Makes about 5 dozen.

DUTCH NEW YEAR'S COOKIES

3 c. flour, sifted
1 Tbsp. baking powder
1/2 tsp. salt
1 tsp. nutmeg
2 eggs
1 c. sugar
1 c. whipping cream
1 1/2 Tbsp. caraway seeds

Sift together flour, baking powder, salt and nutmeg. Set aside. Beat eggs until very light. Beat in sugar, a little at a time, and cream until smooth. Stir in flour combination and caraway seeds.

Refrigerate several hours until dough is firm enough to handle. Roll about 1/4" thick on lightly floured board. Cut with a small cookie cutter. Sprinkle tops with sugar and bake on greased cookie sheet in 350 oven for 10 minutes. Makes about 4 dozen.

CHOCOLATE SHOT COOKIES

1 c. butter
1 c. powdered sugar
1 tsp. vanilla
1 1/4 c. flour
1 c. oatmeal
Chocolate shots

Cream butter and sugar. Add rest of ingredients. Refrigerate 1/2 hour. Shape into rolls the size of 50 cent pieces and coat with chocolate shots. Refrigerate at least 1 hour. Slice. Bake at 325 for 10-15 minutes.

CHOCOLATE SNOWBALLS

1 1/4 c. margarine
2/3 c. sugar
1 tsp. vanilla
2 c. flour
1/4 tsp. salt
1/2 c. cocoa
2 c. nuts, finely chopped

Cream margarine and sugar. Add remaining ingredients. Mix well, cover and chill. Make balls the size of walnuts. Bake on ungreased baking sheet at 350 for 20 minutes. Cool and coat with powdered sugar.

🌲 🌲 🌲 🌲 🌲

ENGLISH WALNUT COOKIES

1 c. margarine
2 c. brown sugar
2 eggs
2 tsp. vanilla
1/2 tsp. salt
2 c. flour
1 tsp. soda
2 c. walnut pieces
1/2 c. Maraschino cherries, chopped

Cream margarine and sugar; beat until smooth. Blend in flour, soda and salt. Stir in nuts and cherries. Form into two 16" long rolls. Wrap in waxed paper. Refrigerate overnight. Cut into 1/4" slices. Place on un-greased cookie sheets. Bake at 375 for 8-10 minutes. Makes 6 dozen.

FRUIT CAKE COOKIES

1 1/2 c. golden raisins
1/4 c. diced citron
1/2 1b. candied cherries, chopped
1/4 c. rum
1/2 c. butter, softened
1/2 c. brown sugar, packed
2 eggs
1 1/2 c. unsifted flour
1/2 tsp. baking soda
2 tsp. cinnamon
1/2 tsp. ground cloves
1/2 tsp. nutmeg
1/8 t. salt
1/2 lb. pecans, chopped
Confectioners' sugar

Soak raisins, citron and cherries in rum for 1 hour. Cream the butter. Add sugar and eggs. Beat until fluffy. Sift flour with baking soda, spices and salt. Add to the butter mixture. Add nuts and rum-soaked fruit. Cover and refrigerate overnight. Form batter into balls. Bake at 325 for 10-12 minutes on greased cookie sheets. Cool. Sprinkle with confectioners' sugar. Makes 7 dozen.

🌲 🌲 🌲 🌲 🌲

CANDY CANE COOKIES

1/2 c. margarine, softened
1/2 c. shortening
1 c. confectioners' sugar
1 egg
1 1/2 tsp. almond extract
1 tsp. vanilla
2 1/2 c. all-purpose flour
1 tsp. salt
1/2 tsp. red food coloring

Heat oven to 375. Mix margarine, shortening, confectioners' sugar, egg and flavorings thoroughly. Blend in flour and salt. Add food coloring to give red (marbled) texture. Shape 1 tsp. of dough into 4" rope and shape into candy cane by rolling back and forth on lightly floured board or put in cookie press. Bake about 9 minutes. Remove from baking sheet when cooled. Makes 4 dozen cookies.

DATE FILLED COOKIES

1 c. sugar
1 egg
1/2 c. sour milk
Pinch salt
1 tsp. soda
1 tsp. baking powder
2 c. flour
2 c. oatmeal, ground in food chopper

Mix ingredients and chill. Roll thin and cut rounds or shapes. Spread filling between two cut cookies; press edges together. Bake on greased cookie sheet at 350 until edges are slightly browned for 10-15 minutes.

Filling:
1 lb. dates, chopped
1 c. sugar
1 c. water
1 c. nuts, chopped

Cook in saucepan until thick. Cool.

ROSETTE COOKIES

2 eggs, slightly beaten
2 tsp. sugar
1 c. milk
1 c. flour
1/4 tsp. salt
1 Tbsp. lemon extract (vanilla, brandy,
    anise or rum extracts can be used)

Sift flour with salt. Add sugar to eggs. Add milk. Stir into egg mixture and beat until it is about the consistency of heavy cream. Add flavoring. Fry.

To fry:

Place approximately 2" oil in deep fryer or saucepan. Heat to 375. Use 2 molds on rosette iron. Heat iron in oil. Dip in batter which has been placed in a bread pan. Do not get batter on top of mold. Immerse completely in hot oil until golden brown or until bubbling stops. Lift iron out. Tap iron gently with wooden spoon. Sprinkle cookies with powdered sugar when cool.

CHOCOLATE ALMOND BUTTERBALLS

2 squares semi-sweet chocolate
   or 1/3 c. semi-sweet chocolate chips
2 Tbsp. milk
1/2 c. sugar
1/4 tsp. salt
3/4 c. butter or margarine, softened
2 tsp. vanilla
1 egg
2 c. flour
1/2 c. almonds, chopped
sugar

Preheat oven to 350. Melt chocolate with milk over low heat; cool. In large bowl, combine chocolate, sugar, salt, butter, vanilla and egg. Beat 2 minutes at medium speed. Stir in flour and nuts. Shape into 1" balls; roll in sugar. Place 2" apart on ungreased cookie sheets. Bake 11-14 minutes until set, but not brown. Frost if desired. Makes about 4 dozen cookies.

COTTAGE CHEESE COOKIES

1 c. shortening
1 c. sugar
3/4 c. brown sugar
1 c. cottage cheese
2 3/4 c. flour
1 tsp. baking powder
1/2 tsp. salt
1/2 tsp. soda
1/2 c. nuts, chopped

Combine ingredients. Chill overnight. Roll into small balls and roll in powdered sugar. Bake on greased cookie sheets at 350 for 11 minutes.

CREAM CHEESE DAINTIES

1/2 c. butter or margarine
1 3-oz. package cream cheese, softened
1/2 c. sugar
1/4 tsp. almond extract
1 c. flour
2 tsp. baking powder
1/4 tsp. salt
1 1/4 c. rice krispies, coarsely crushed
Drained Maraschino cherries

Cream together butter or margarine, cream cheese, sugar and almond extract until light. Sift flour, baking powder and salt. Stir into margarine mixture just until combined. Chill 1 to 2 hours. Shape into marble-sized balls and roll in crushed cereal. Place on ungreased cookie sheet. Top each with 1/2 Maraschino cherry. Bake at 350 for 12-15 minutes. Makes 4 dozen.

CHOCOLATE CRINKLES

1/2 c. shortening
1 2/3 c. granulated sugar
2 tsp. vanilla
2 eggs
2 1-oz. squares unsweetened chocolate, melted
2 c. sifted enriched flour
2 tsp. baking powder
1/2 tsp. salt
1/3 c. milk
1/2 c. walnuts, chopped
Confectioners' sugar, sifted

Thoroughly cream shortening, sugar and vanilla. Beat in eggs and chocolate. Sift together dry ingredients. Blend in alternately with milk. Add nuts. Chill 3 hours. Form into 1" balls. Roll in confectioners' sugar. Place on greased cookie sheet 2-3" apart. Bake at 350 for about 15 minutes. Makes 4 dozen cookies.

PECAN SANDIES

1 c. butter or margarine
1/3 c. granulated sugar
2 tsp. water
2 tsp. vanilla
2 c. all-purpose flour, sifted
1 c. pecans, chopped

Cream butter and sugar. Add water and vanilla and mix well. Blend in flour and nuts. Chill 4 hours. Shape into balls or fingers. Bake on ungreased cookie sheet at 325 for about 20 minutes. Remove from pan. Cool slightly. Roll in confectioners' sugar. Makes 3 dozen cookies.

🌲 🌲 🌲 🌲 🌲

CHERRY WINKS

2 1/4 c. flour
1 tsp. baking powder
1/2 tsp. salt
3/4 c. shortening
2 eggs
2 Tbsp. milk
1/2 tsp. soda
1 c. sugar
1 c. dates
1 tsp. vanilla
1 c. pecans
1/3 c. Maraschino cherries, chopped
2 1/2 c. corn flakes

Sift dry ingredients together and set aside. Cream sugar and shortening. Add eggs, vanilla and milk. Mix well. Add dry ingredients. Add pecans, dates and cherries. Mix well. Shape dough into balls, using level tablespoons. Roll each cookie in corn flakes. Place on cookie sheet; top with 1/4 Maraschino cherry. Bake at 375 for 10 minutes.

GRANDMA'S CRACKLE TOPS

2 3/4 c. flour
2 tsp. baking soda
1/2 tsp. salt
2 tsp. pumpkin pie spice
3/4 c. butter or margarine
3/4 c. sugar
1/2 c. molasses
1 egg
1 tsp. vanilla
Granulated sugar

Sift flour, baking soda, salt and pumpkin pie spice onto waxed paper. Beat butter and 3/4 c. sugar until light and fluffy in large bowl with electric mixer on high speed. Beat in molasses and egg until smooth. Stir in vanilla. Blend in flour mixture to make a soft dough. Cover bowl with plastic wrap and refrigerate 4 hours. Sprinkle granulated sugar on waxed paper. Roll dough into 1" balls and roll in sugar. Place balls, 3" apart, on ungreased cookie sheets. Flatten with bottom of glass dipped in sugar. Sprinkle cookies with few drops water. (This gives the crackle tops.) Bake at 375 for 10 minutes or until cookies are firm, but not hard. Cool. Store in metal tin with tight cover. Makes 5 dozen.

PEPPERNUTS

This recipe is written in batches.

2-3-4 c. sugar
1/2-3/4-1 c. butter
1/4-1/3-1/2 c. molasses
1-2-3 eggs
1-1 1/2-2 c. water
6-9-12 c. flour
3-4 1/2-6 tsp. baking powder
1-1 1/2-2 tsp. cinnamon
1/2-3/4-1 tsp. cloves
1/2-3/4-1 tsp. red (cayenne) pepper

Mix all ingredients together. Add 2 cups of flour so dough is not sticky.. Put lots of flour on table and pat out dough to 1/4" thick. Cut in long strips 1/2" wide then in squares 1/2" wide, keeping flour on dough at all times to keep from sticking. Lift into sieve with pancake turner to shake off excess flour. BE GENTLE!! Bake on ungreased cookie sheet at 400 for 10-12 minutes. Do not let them touch.

ALMOND BUTTER BALLS

2 c. flour, sifted
1/2 tsp. salt
1 c. butter or margarine, softened
1/4 c. honey
3/4 tsp. almond extract
1 1/2 c. blanched almonds, finely chopped

Stir together flour and salt. Work butter in bowl until creamy. Add honey and beat well. Add almond extract. Gradually add dry ingredients. Beat well. Add nuts. Cover and chill 1 hour. Heat oven to 350. Shape dough into 1" balls and put on ungreased cookie sheet about 1 1/2" apart. Bake for 12-15 minutes or until lightly browned. Roll in powdered sugar while still warm and again when cool.

🌲 🌲 🌲 🌲 🌲

DATE-NUT RAISIN COOKIES

1 c. flour
1 tsp. baking powder
1/4 tsp. salt
1/2 c. butter, softened
1 c. nuts, chopped
1 c. coconut
1/2 c. dates, cut up
1/2 c. raisins
1 egg
vanilla to taste

Mix all dry ingredients together. Cut in butter until particles are pea sized. Stir in nuts, coconut, dates, raisins, egg and vanilla. Mix dough until it forms a ball. Chill one hour. Shape into balls and place 1/2" apart on greased cookie sheet. With tines of fork flatten balls. Bake at 350 for 15 minutes. Makes 48 cookies.

CITRONS

On Christmas Eve the "reveillon", the late supper that is the culinary high point of the season in France, may have ended with these tangy little cookies.

1/2 c. butter or margarine
1/2 c. sugar
1 tsp. lemon extract
1 Tbsp. grated lemon rind
2 c. all-purpose flour
1/2 tsp. salt
1/4 c. lemon juice
1/4 c. milk
Confectioners' sugar

In mixing bowl, cream together butter and sugar. Add lemon extract and grated lemon rind. Set aside. Sift together flour and salt. Add dry ingredients to butter mixture, beating until mixture is crumb-like. Beat in lemon juice and milk. Chill dough at least 4 hours. Roll dough into small balls and place on lightly greased cookie sheets. Bake at 400 for 10-20 minutes. While still hot, roll in confectioners' sugar. Cool. Roll in sugar again. Makes about 4 dozen cookies.

🌲 🌲 🌲 🌲 🌲

SPRITZ COOKIES (Sweden)

1 lb. butter, no substitute
1 c. sugar
1 egg, well beaten
1 tsp. vanilla
4 c. flour, sifted

Preheat oven to 400; use top rack. Cream softened butter thoroughly; add sugar gradually and cream until light and fluffy. Add egg and beat well; add vanilla. Add sifted flour gradually to mixture. Beat well after each addition of flour; work in all flour. Put dough through cookie press in desired shapes. Bake on ungreased cookie sheet 4-5 minutes or until bottom is brown. Makes 100 cookies.

GINGER SNAPS

3/4 c. shortening
1 c. sugar
1/4 c. molasses
1 egg
2 c. flour
1 tsp. cloves
1 tsp. cinnamon
1 tsp. ginger
2 tsp. soda
1/2 tsp. salt

Cream shortening and sugar. Add molasses and egg. Beat well. Add sifted dry ingredients. Mix well. Roll into small balls, and dip in sugar. Place on greased cookie sheet. Bake at 350 for 15 minutes. Do not overbake. Makes 4 dozen.

SOUR CREAM TARTS

1/2 lb. butter
1 1/2 c. flour
1/2 c. sour cream

Mix flour and butter as for pie crust. Add sour cream. Roll and cut 2 little rounds. Cut a hole in center of one and stack together. Fill hole with peach jam. Sprinkle sugar mixed with a dash of water around the edge. Bake at 350 for 15-20 minutes.

CHOCOLATE MINT SURPRISE COOKIES

1 c. butter or margarine
1 c. granulated sugar
1/2 c. brown sugar, firmly packed
2 eggs, unbeaten
1 tsp. vanilla
3 c. flour
1 tsp. soda
1/2 tsp. salt
2 7-oz. boxes Bavarian solid chocolate mint candies
    (about 1/2" square with no filling)
Walnut or pecan halves

Thoroughly cream together the butter, granulated sugar and brown sugar; add eggs and vanilla. Mix well. Sift together the flour, soda and salt. Refrigerate dough, covered, for one hour. Shape a generous tablespoon of dough around each piece of candy. Roll between palms of hands into balls; place 2-3" apart on ungreased baking sheet Cookies will flatten while baking. Decorate with walnut or pecan halves. Bake in 375 oven for 12-15 minutes or until cookies are golden brown around the edges. Makes 3 dozen cookies. These freeze nicely. To double this recipe, 3 boxes of mint candies will be needed.

PEANUT BUTTER KISSES

1 3/4 c. flour
1 tsp. baking soda
1/4 tsp. salt
1/2 c. sugar
1/2 c. light brown sugar
1/2 c. margarine
1/2 c. creamy peanut butter
1 egg
2 Tbsp. milk
2 tsp. vanilla
4-5 dozen chocolate stars or kisses

Stir soda, flour and salt. Add all other ingredients except chocolate stars or kisses. Chill dough 30 minutes. Preheat oven to 375. Roll small amount of dough into 1" balls. Place on ungreased cookie sheet and bake 10-12 minutes or until lightly browned. Remove and IMMEDIATELY press chocolate star into center. Cookie will crack around the edge. Makes 4-5 dozen.

MACADAMIA NUT TARTS

Spice Tart Pastry:
- 1 1/2 c. flour
- 2 Tbsp. sugar
- 1/2 tsp. salt
- 1/4 tsp. ground nutmeg
- 1/4 tsp. ground cinnamon
- 1/3 c. unsalted sweet butter
- 2-3 Tbsp. orange juice

Combine flour, sugar, salt and spices in medium size bowl; cut in butter until mixture resembles coarse crumbs. Stir in orange juice, 1 Tbsp. at a time, until flour is moistened and dough almost cleans side of bowl. Gather dough into ball. Refrigerate, wrapped in waxed paper, 1 hour. Press about 2 tsp. of dough into each 2" tart pan. Chill 30 minutes.

Filling:
- 1 egg
- 1/2 c. light corn syrup
- 2/3 c. sugar
- 1 1/2 tsp. butter or margarine, softened
- 1 Tbsp. flour
- 1/2 tsp. vanilla
- 1/8 tsp. salt
- 5-oz. can macadamia nuts, chopped

Heat oven to 350. Beat egg until thick and lemon colored in small bowl; beat in corn syrup, sugar, butter, flour, vanilla and salt. Stir in nuts. Spoon 1 tsp. of filling into each pastry shell. Bake until top is golden and bubbly, 12-15 minutes. Cool completely. Can be stored, covered with aluminum foil, in freezer for up to two months.

Hint

To freeze cookie dough, wrap tightly in plastic wrap. It is easier to divide into two or three units. Wrap again in freezer wrap or heavy aluminum foil. Well wrapped dough can be kept frozen for up to a month.

RAISIN-FILLED COOKIES

4 c. flour
1 tsp. baking powder
1/2 tsp. salt
1 tsp. baking soda
1/4 tsp. nutmeg
1 c. sugar
1 c. brown sugar, packed
1 c. butter
3 eggs
2 tsp. vanilla
raisin filling

1. Mix flour, baking powder, soda, salt and nutmeg.
2. Thoroughly mix sugars; with pastry blender cut in butter until fine particles form.
3. Beat eggs with vanilla.
4. Mix 1, 2, and 3 together until it forms a smooth dough.
5. Chill several hours or overnight.
6. Divide dough into several portions. Work with one at a time. Keep rest in refrigerator.
7. On floured pastry cloth, roll dough to 1/8". Cut out 2" circles.
8. Put scant teaspoonful of filling in center of half the circle. Put tops on. Press edges together with fork.
9. Bake 1 1/2" apart on ungreased cookie sheet at 375 for 10-12 minutes.
10. Sprinkle with powdered sugar.

Raisin Filling:
1. Mix 3/4 c. sugar and 1 tsp. cornstarch.
2. Heat 1 c. water and 2 c. raisins to boiling.
3. Add sugar mixture, boil gently and stir until liquid is clear and slightly thick.
4. Stir in 1 tsp. vanilla.

ALMOND CRESCENTS

1/2 lb. butter, softened
2/3 c. sugar
2 c. flour
1 1/2 c. almonds, ground
1 tsp. vanilla extract
3/4 c. powdered sugar

1. Cream butter and sugar together. Add flour. Mix well. Stir in nuts and vanilla and mix well. Shape into a big ball and wrap in plastic wrap. Refrigerate 1 hour.
2. Grease cookie sheet.
3. To make cookies, pinch off enough to make a ball 1 1/4" in diameter. Roll ball in palms into a 1/2" thick strip and taper ends. Place on cookie sheet and shape into crescent.
4. Bake at 350 for 15-20 minutes. Makes 3 dozen.
5. Let cookies cool on the baking sheet for a few minutes before transferring to a wire rack. Sift powdered sugar over them while still warm.

🌲 🌲 🌲 🌲 🌲

CHRISTMAS FRUIT COOKIES

1 c. butter
1 c. brown sugar
2 eggs
1 tsp. vanilla
1 c. dates, chopped
1/2 c. candied cherries
1/2 c. pecans, chopped
4 c. flour
1 tsp. salt
1 tsp. soda
1 tsp. cream of tartar

Cream butter and sugar; add eggs and beat well. Add vanilla, dates, cherries and nuts. Sift dry ingredients; gradually add to creamed mixture until a stiff dough is formed. Shape into three rolls; wrap in waxed paper and store in refrigerator at least 8 hours. Slice and bake at 425 for 9 minutes. Makes 4 dozen.

COCONUT MINT COOKIES

2 c. sugar
1 c. butter or margarine
2 eggs
1 tsp. vanilla
3 c. flour
1/2 tsp. salt
1/2 tsp. soda
1/2 tsp. cream of tartar
1 c. quick oats
1/2 c. pecans, chopped
1 3 1/2-oz. can flaked coconut
Mint jelly

Cream butter and sugar. Beat in eggs and vanilla. Stir in flour, salt, soda and cream of tartar. Stir in oats and pecans. Cover and chill 2-3 hours. Shape into 1" balls and roll in coconut. Place on greased cookie sheet. Make an indention on top of each cookie. Bake at 375 for 10-12 minutes. Remove cookies and cool on wire rack. Fill each with about 1/4 tsp. mint jelly.

TEA TIME TASSIES

1 3-oz. package cream cheese
1/2 c. butter or margarine
1 c. sifted flour
3/4 c. brown sugar
1 Tbsp. butter or margarine, softened
1 tsp. vanilla
Dash salt
2/3 c. pecans, coarsely chopped

Cheese Pastry:
Let cream cheese and 1/2 c. butter soften to room temperature. Blend. Stir in flour. Chill about 1 hour. Shape into 2 dozen 1" balls. Place in tiny ungreased 1 3/4" muffin cups. Press onto bottom and sides of cups.

Pecan Filling:
Beat together egg, sugar, 1 Tbsp. butter, vanilla and salt just until smooth. Divide 1/2 of pecans among pastry-lined cups. Add egg mixture and top with remaining pecans. Bake in 325 oven for 25 minutes or until filling is set. Cool and remove from tins. Makes 2 dozen.

ALMOND RAVIOLI COOKIES

1 1/2 c. powdered sugar
1 c. butter or margarine at room temperature
1 egg
1 tsp. vanilla
2 1/2 c. all-purpose flour
1 tsp. soda
1 tsp. cream or tartar
About 2/3 c. almond paste
About 1/3 c. sliced almonds

Beat together sugar and butter until fluffy. Blend in egg and vanilla. Mix flour with soda and cream of tartar; blend with creamed mixture. Divide dough in half. Wrap and chill until firm, up to 24 hours. Place one portion of dough between two pieces of waxed paper (each about 20" long) and roll to make a 10" × 15" rectangle (if dough becomes too soft, chill until firm). Peel off and discard top paper. With a pastry wheel or long- bladed knife, lightly mark dough into 1" squares. Place a small ball of almond paste (a scant 1/4 tsp. for each) in the center of each square; chill while rolling top layer.

Repeat rolling procedure for second portion of dough. Peel off and discard the top paper; invert onto almond-topped dough. Peel off and discard paper. Gently press top layer of dough around filling.

Flour a pastry wheel or knife and cut filled dough into 1" squares. Run pastry wheel around outer edges to seal (or press with fingers).

Place cookies about 1" apart on ungreased 12'×'15" baking sheets. Push a sliced almond diagonally into the center of each cookie. Bake at 350 until golden, 10-12 minutes. Cool cookies on wire racks. Store airtight at room temperature up to 1 week. Freeze for longer storage. Makes about 12 dozen cookies.

Hint

To thaw frozen cookie dough, remove from freezer 1-2 hours before you plan to slice and bake it. Put in refrigerator. Swirled cookies containing a filling may take a little longer to thaw.

SOUR CREAM SUGAR COOKIES

2 c. sugar
1 c. butter
1 c. sour cream
1 tsp. vanilla
2 eggs
1 tsp. soda dissolved in 1 Tbsp. water
1 tsp. baking powder
4-5 c. flour, or enough to make stiff dough

Mix all ingredients. Chill for 1 hour or more. Roll fairly thick. Cut into desired shapes. Bake at 375 for 8-10 minutes.

🌲 🌲 🌲 🌲 🌲

LEMON CHEESE LOGS

1 c. sugar
1 c. butter or margarine, softened
3 oz. cream cheese, softened
1 egg yolk
2 1/2 c. all-purpose flour
1 c. walnuts, finely chopped
1/2 tsp. salt
1/2 tsp. grated lemon peel
6 oz. semi-sweet chocolate chips, melted

Cream sugar, butter and cream cheese in large mixing bowl until light and fluffy. Beat in egg yolk. Stir in flour, walnuts, salt and lemon peel. Refrigerate covered at least 2 hours.

Heat oven to 325. Shape about 1 Tbsp. of the dough into a log, 1" long. Repeat with remaining dough. Place on ungreased baking sheets. Bake until brown, about 12 minutes. Cool on wire racks. Dip ends of logs in chocolate; dip chocolate-coated ends into decorating sprinkles. Let stand on wire racks until chocolate sets. Store between layers of waxed paper in airtight containers at room temperature no longer then 10 days or in freezer no long than 3 months.

MELTING MOMENTS COOKIES

1 c. butter
1/2 c. powdered sugar
1 1/4 c. all-purpose flour
1/2 c. cornstarch
1/2 tsp. almond extract

Cream butter and powdered sugar. Beat until light and fluffy. Combine flour and cornstarch. Add flour mixture and extract. Beat until well blended. Shape dough into 1" balls. Flatten with the bottom of a floured glass. Bake 20 minutes in 300 oven. Let stand a few minutes before removing to wire rack to cool. Frost if desired.

♠ ♠ ♠ ♠ ♠

FINNISH FINGERS

2 c. butter or margarine
1 c. brown sugar, packed
2 eggs
2 tsp. vanilla
5 1/3 c. flour
2 tsp. baking powder
1/4 c. sugar
1/4 tsp. cinnamon
1 egg white, slightly beaten
1 c. semi-sweet chocolate chips, melted

In a mixer bowl, thoroughly cream together butter or margarine and brown sugar. Beat in eggs and vanilla. Thoroughly stir together flour and baking powder; add gradually to creamed mixture, mixing until smooth. Do not chill. Roll dough into 2 1/2" fingers, using a scant tablespoon of dough for each finger.

Dip the top of each finger into egg white, then into the sugar-cinnamon mixture. Place sugar side up on greased cookie sheet. Bake in 350 oven for 10 minutes or until bottom is lightly browned. Remove from cookie sheets to wire racks to cool. Dip one end into melted chocolate and place on waxed paper until chocolate hardens. Makes 100 cookies.

UTTERLY DUDLEYS (Pecan goodies)

These are like small pecan pies.

Pastry:
>   2 sticks margarine, softened
>   2 3-oz. packages cream cheese, softened
>   2 c. flour

Cream margarine and cream cheese together. Add flour, 1/2 c. at a time. Chill. Pinch off small balls and press into very small muffin tins.

Filling:
>   1 c. pecans, coarsely ground
>   2 eggs
>   1 1/2 c. light brown sugar
>   2 Tbsp. butter
>   dash salt
>   1/4 tsp. vanilla

Sprinkle part of the pecans on unbaked dough in muffin tins. Beat eggs. Add remaining ingredients except pecans. Spoon about 1 1/2 tsp. mixture into muffin tins. Sprinkle rest of pecans over filling. Bake at 350 for 15-17 minutes. Reduce heat to 250 and bake for 10 minutes more. Cool before removing from pans. Makes about 6 dozen cookies.

🌲 🌲 🌲 🌲 🌲

FRENCH CHERIE CAKES

Basic dough:
>   1 c. butter or margarine, softened
>   1 1/2 c. confectioners' sugar
>   1 egg
>   1 tsp. vanilla
>   2 1/2 c. flour

Mix butter, sugar, egg and vanilla thoroughly. Blend in flour; divide dough in half. To half of the mixture add 1 c. of finely chopped red candied cherries. Cover and chill at least 2 hours.

Heat oven to 375. Roll dough 1/8" thick on well-floured board. Cut into 2" circles or scalloped rounds. Cut small hole in center of half of the rounds. Bake on ungreased baking sheet 8-10 minutes. Cool. Spread plain rounds with filling.

Filling:
2 c. confectioners' sugar
1 tsp. almond extract
1 1/2-2 Tbsp. milk
Few drops food coloring, if desired
Blend together. Top each plain round with filling and cut-out round. Makes 2 dozen.

CHOCOLATE SNOWBALLS I

Vanilla sugar:
  1 Tbsp. vanilla
  1 c. powdered sugar
Mix and press through sieve and set aside.
  1/2 c. plus 3 Tbsp. butter
    or margarine
  1/4 c. evaporated milk
  1 tsp. vanilla

  1 3/4 c. flour
  2 Tbsp. cocoa
  1/2 c. powdered sugar
  1 c. nuts, finely chopped

Cream butter until light. Beat in milk. Add 1 tsp. vanilla. Sift dry ingredients and gradually add to creamed mixture. Mix in nuts. Chill. Form into small balls. Place 2" apart on greased baking sheet. Bake at 325 for 20 minutes. Roll in vanilla sugar.

Hint

Make your own VANILLA SUGAR:
Either confectioners' sugar or granulated sugar can be used. Vanilla sugar can be used in place of plain sugar in a recipe or used to sprinkle over berries, fruits or to flavor whipped cream.
Split a vanilla bean in half lengthwise. Place both halves in a tall jar with 1-2 c. granulated sugar. Cover and let stand for at least 24 hours. Replace any sugar used from container. Vanilla bean will continue to flavor sugar up to a year.

SWEET PRETZELS

4 c. flour
1 1/2 c. butter or margarine, softened
1 c. sugar
2 large eggs
White of 1 large egg
Yolk of 1 large egg
1 tsp. vanilla
1 tsp. freshly grated lemon peel
Colored sugar

Put all ingredients except egg white and colored sugar in a large bowl and beat with mixer until thoroughly mixed. Cover dough and chill 1 hour or until firm enough to shape. Form dough into round shape and cut into 5 wedges. Roll each wedge into a cylinder and cut into 12 pieces. Heat oven to 350. On lightly floured surface roll each piece of dough into 7" rope. Twist into pretzel shape and bake 1" apart on ungreased baking sheet for 15 minutes. Let cool 5 minutes. Brush lightly with egg white and sprinkle with sugar. Bake 2 minutes more. Cool on wire rack. Makes 5 dozen cookies.

🌲 🌲 🌲 🌲 🌲

CHOCOLATE CRINKLE COOKIES

2 c. flour
1 c. sugar
4 squares unsweetened baking chocolate
4 Tbsp. unsalted butter
4 large eggs
2 tsp. baking powder
1/2 tsp. salt
1/2 c. powdered sugar

Melt chocolate and butter together. Cool. Beat all ingredients except powdered sugar together with electric mixer until smooth. Chill until firm. Heat oven to 350. Shape rounded teaspoonfuls of dough into balls; roll in powdered sugar. Place 1 1/2" apart on greased baking sheets. Bake for 10 minutes, or until cookies crack and feel firm when pressed gently. Cool. Makes 6 dozen cookies.

"GREAT" SUGAR COOKIES

Cream together:
    1 c. margarine
    1 c. powdered sugar
    1 c. granulated sugar
Add:
    2 eggs
    1 tsp. soda
    1 tsp. cream of tartar
    1/2 tsp. salt
    4 1/2 c. flour
    1 c. oil
    1 tsp. vanilla
Mix thoroughly and roll into tiny balls. Flatten with glass dipped in sugar.
Bake at 350 for 10-12 minutes.

🌲   🌲   🌲   🌲   🌲

BROWN-EYED SUSANS

    3/4 c. margarine
    1/2 c. sugar
    1 egg
    1 tsp. vanilla
    1 2/3 c. flour
    1/4 tsp. salt
    Chocolate filling
    Almonds as garnish
Cream margarine, sugar, egg and vanilla in small mixer bowl until fluffy.
Add flour and salt. Blend well. Chill if too soft to handle. Shape small
portion of dough into 1" balls. Place on ungreased baking sheet. Make
indentation in center with thumb. Bake at 375 for 8-10 minutes or until
firm and lightly browned.

Filling:
    1 c. confectioners' sugar
    3 Tbsp. cocoa
    2 Tbsp. margarine
    1/2 tsp. vanilla
    1 1/2 Tbsp. milk
Blend until smooth and creamy.
Fill each cookie with teaspoonful of chocolate filling. Swirl with spatula;
top with an almond. Remove from cookie sheet onto a rack to cool.
Makes about 3 dozen cookies.

APRICOT FOLDOVERS

2 6-oz. packages dried apricots
1/2 c. apricot brandy
3/4 c. butter
1 1/2 c. flour
1/4 c. sugar
1/4 tsp. ground allspice
1 egg yolk, beaten
1/3 c. dairy sour cream

Soak apricots in 1/2 c. brandy for 1 hour or overnight. Drain and reserve liquid. Pat apricots dry.

In mixing bowl combine flour, sugar and allspice. Cut in butter until mixture resembles fine crumbs. Combine egg yolk and sour cream. Blend into flour mixture. Cover and chill several hours or overnight. Divide into 2 equal portions; keep chilled until ready to use. On lightly floured surface, roll out 1/2 of the dough to 1/8" thickness. Cut with 2 1/2" fluted round cutter. Place each cookie on ungreased cookie sheet. Place one apricot on one half of each cookie. Fold over other half, leaving apricot showing. Bake in 350 oven about 12 minutes until lightly browned. Remove and cool. Dip in Apricot Brandy Icing.

Apricot Brandy Icing:
    1 c. sifted powdered sugar
    2-3 Tbsp. of reserved apricot brandy
Combine. Should be of thin consistency.

ANGEL FOOD COOKIES

1 c. shortening
1/2 c. brown sugar
1/2 c. white sugar
1 egg, beaten
1/4 tsp. salt
2 c. flour
1 tsp. soda
1 tsp. cream of tartar
1 c. coconut
1 tsp. banana flavoring

Mix in order given. Roll into small balls. Dip top into water, then into sugar. Bake on greased cookie sheets at 375 for 15 minutes.

CHOCOLATE SURPRISE COOKIES

This is a rather expensive cookie only made for special occasions, but they are extra good!!

1 1/2 c. margarine
1 c. sugar
2 eggs, beaten
1 tsp. vanilla
1 tsp. mint flavoring
1/2 tsp. salt
2 tsp. baking powder
3 1/2 c. flour
1 8-oz. package chocolate candy wafers
     (available at craft stores or candy making supply stores.

Cream margarine, sugar, eggs, vanilla, mint flavoring and salt. Stir in flour and baking powder. Mix well. Chill dough 1 hour or more. Shape into 1" balls. Flatten and place candy wafer in center; bring dough up around to encase wafer. Place 2" apart on lightly greased cookie sheet. Bake at 350 for 10-12 minutes. Remove immediately from cookie sheet. Cool and store.

🌲 🌲 🌲 🌲 🌲

REFRIGERATOR COOKIES

3 c. sifted flour
1 1/2 tsp. baking powder
1/2 tsp. salt
3/4 c. butter or margarine
1 c. granulated sugar or light brown sugar, packed
2 eggs
2 tsp. vanilla
1 c. M & M's, finely chopped

Combine and sift flour, baking powder and salt. Cream butter well. Add sugar and cream well. Add eggs and vanilla. Cream until light and fluffy. Stir in dry ingredients just until well blended. Divide dough into 2 equal portions. Chill until dough can be shaped into rolls about 8" long. Roll in waxed paper or foil. Close ends; chill thoroughly. Slice about 1/8" thick Place on ungreased baking sheet. Sprinkle with chopped candies. Bake at 375 for 6-8 minutes. Makes 6-8 dozen.

DATE PINWHEELS

Cook together until thick and set aside:
  1 1/3 c. dates, chopped
  2/3 c. sugar
  2/3 c. water
  2/3 c. nuts
Cream together:
  2/3 c. shortening
  1 1/2 c. brown sugar
Add:
  2 eggs
Add to creamed mixture and blend well:
  2 2/3 c. flour
  1/2 tsp. salt
  1/2 tsp. soda
Divide dough into 3 or 4 parts and chill. Roll out and spread with date filling. Roll up and wrap in wax paper. Chill overnight or freeze. Slice and place on greased cookie sheet. Bake at 375 for 8-10 minutes or until light brown. Makes about 5 dozen.

LEMON FROSTED PECAN COOKIES

  1 c. butter or margarine
  3/4 c. powdered sugar
  2 Tbsp. milk
  1 1/2 c. all-purpose flour
  3/4 c. corn starch
  3/4 c. pecans
Stir butter to soften. Add powdered sugar, milk, flour and cornstarch. Cream until well blended. Chill. Place small spoonfuls of chopped pecans 2" apart on an ungreased baking sheet. Shape dough into small balls and flatten each over a pile of pecans. Bake at 350 for 12-15 minutes. Cool and frost.

Frosting:
  2 1/2 c. powdered sugar
  1 Tbsp. butter or margarine
  3 Tbsp. lemon juice
  few drops yellow food coloring
Mix together until smooth and frost cookies.

GRANDMA'S SUGAR COOKIES

2 c. sugar
1 c. shortening
1 c. thick sour cream
2 eggs
2 1/4 c. flour
1 tsp. soda
Vanilla to taste
Pinch of salt

Mix all ingredients (the dough will be soft). Chill. Can be refrigerated for several weeks to be used as needed. Roll out on floured surface. Cut out favorite shapes. Bake at 375 for 5-10 minutes. Watch closely.

SNICKERDOODLES

1/2 c. butter or margarine
1/2 c. shortening
1 1/2 c. sugar
2 eggs
2 3/4 c. flour
2 tsp. cream of tartar
1 tsp. soda
1/4 tsp. salt

Mix thoroughly butter, shortening, sugar and eggs. Blend in flour, cream of tartar, soda and salt. Shape dough by rounded teaspoonfuls into balls. Mix 2 Tbsp. sugar* and 2 tsp. cinnamon together. Roll balls of dough into mixture. Place on ungreased cookie sheets. Bake at 400 for 8-10 minutes.

*At Christmas time, use colored sugar.

FROZEN FRUIT COOKIES

1 c. butter or margarine
1 c. confectioners' sugar, sifted
1 egg
2 1/2 c. flour
1/4 tsp. cream of tartar
1/2 c. candied mixed fruit, chopped
1/2 c. pecans, chopped
1 c. whole candied fruit, such as cherries

Cream butter and sugar. Beat in egg. Stir in flour and cream of tartar. Add pecans and fruit. Form into rolls 1-1 1/2" in diameter. Wrap in wax paper. Freeze. Slice rolls into 1/4" sections. Place on greased cookie sheet. Bake at 375 for 6-8 minutes. Makes 10 dozen.

GRANDMA'S KRINGLA (SWEDISH)

1 1/4 c. sugar
1 8-oz. carton sour cream
Few drops vanilla and
 lemon extracts
1 1/2 tsp. baking soda
1 tsp. salt
Couple shakes nutmeg
1/4 c. margarine
3/4 c. buttermilk
3 1/2-4 c. flour
2 1/2 tsp. baking powder

Cream together sugar, sour cream, vanilla and lemon, baking soda, salt, nutmeg, margarine and buttermilk. Add flour.
Refrigerate overnight. Roll small, small amounts in shape of pencil on floured surface. Shape on "Pammed" cookie sheet in shape of pretzel or bow. Bake at 400 for 3-5 minutes. Place under broiler for about 2 minutes or until lightly brown.

ALMOND TARTLETS

1 c. blanched almonds
1 c. butter, softened
1/2 tsp. almond extract
1/2 tsp. lemon extract
2/3 c. sugar
2 egg yolks
2 c. flour, sifted
1 12-oz. jar currant or apricot jelly

Grind almonds in food processor or blender to a fine powder. Beat together butter, extracts, sugar and egg yolks in large bowl with electric mixer until light and fluffy. Add almonds and flour. Beat at low speed until firm dough forms. Preheat oven to 325. Place small cupcake papers in 1" muffin pans (gem pans). Divide dough into 3/4" balls. Press one ball into each cupcake paper to cover sides and bottom, hollowing out center to form tartlet. Bake in preheated oven at 325 for 20-25 minutes or until edges are golden. Remove from pans and cool completely on wire racks. Spoon about 1/2 tsp. jelly or preserves into each tart. If tartlets are to be stored for several days, do not fill them until ready to serve.

🌲 🌲 🌲 🌲 🌲

ALMOND BUTTER COOKIES - QURENBEDIES

1 lb. butter
1 c. almonds
2 tsp. orange juice
2 tsp. vanilla
4 c. flour (start with this and add more
    to get a soft, workable dough)
1 c. powdered sugar
2 egg yolks
2 tsp. anisette
1 tsp. baking powder

Melt butter; skim. Cream with powdered sugar. Mix baking powder with orange juice and add with eggs and other flavorings. Add almonds and enough flour to make a soft, manageable dough. Shape into balls. Bake at 375 for 15 minutes. Dip in powdered sugar when cooled. Makes about 80 cookies.

CHOCOLATE-COCONUT TASSIES

1 4-oz. package German Sweet Chocolate
1/3 c. butter or margarine
2 3-oz. packages cream cheese
1 c. flour
1/3 c. sugar
2 tsp. vanilla
1 c. flaked coconut
1/2 c. pecans, chopped
Candied cherries, chopped

For Pastry:
Melt half of the chocolate. In a mixer bowl, beat together butter, one package of cream cheese and the melted chocolate. Add flour; beat until combined. Cover and chill at least one hour.

For Filling:
Beat together the remaining package of cream cheese, sugar and vanilla until mixture is smooth. Stir in coconut and pecans.
Shape chilled dough into 30 1" balls; place each ball in an ungreased 1 3/4" muffin cup. Press dough onto bottom and up sides of cups. Spoon about 2 teaspoons filling into each dough lined cup. Top each with a few pieces of chopped cherries. Bake in a 325 oven for 25 minutes or until coconut is light brown. Cool. Remove from pans. Melt remaining chocolate; drizzle on top of each cookie. Store in a covered container. Makes 30 cookies.

🌲　🌲　🌲　🌲　🌲

MEXICAN MOCHA BALLS

1 c. butter or margarine
1/2 c. sugar
1 tsp. vanilla
2 c. flour
1/4 c. unsweetened cocoa powder
1 tsp. instant coffee crystals
1/4 tsp. salt
1 c. walnuts, finely chopped
1/2 c. Maraschino cherries, chopped

Cream butter, sugar and vanilla. Stir flour with cocoa, coffee and salt. Gradually beat into creamed mixture. Stir in nuts and cherries. Chill 1 hour. Form into 1" balls. Place on ungreased baking sheet. Bake at 350 for 20 minutes. Cool on rack. While warm, but not hot, dust with extra fine granulated sugar. Makes 7 dozen.

CHRISTMAS BALLS

1/2 c. sugar
1/4 c. butter
1/4 c. shortening
1 egg
1 tsp. vanilla
1 1/2 c. flour
1/2 tsp. salt
1/4 tsp. soda
Red or green food coloring

Mix sugar, butter, shortening, egg and vanilla. Stir in flour, salt and soda. Stir food coloring into 2/3 of the dough. Refrigerate plain and colored doughs for at least 1 hour. Roll colored dough into balls and wrap plain dough around. Roll in colored sugar. Refrigerate at least 8 hours. Bake on ungreased cookie sheet at 375 until light brown for 7-8 minutes. Makes 4 1/2 dozen cookies.

APRICOT ENVELOPES

Cream cheese pastry:
1 c. all-purpose flour
1/2 tsp. salt
1 c. unsalted butter
1 3-oz. package cream cheese

To make pastry, mix flour and salt in a small bowl. Cut in chilled butter until particles resemble small peas. Mix in cream cheese with fork until blended and mixture forms a dough. Chill at least 1 hour. On lightly floured surface roll out pastry to a 12" square keeping edges even. Cut in 2" squares.

Filling:
1/3 c. apricot preserves
1 tsp. grated lemon peel
1 egg white, slightly beaten
3 Tbsp. minced blanched almonds

For filling, mix apricot preserves and lemon peel. Place 1/2 measuring teaspoonfuls in center of each square. Fold up two opposite corners; pinch to seal. Place 1" apart on lightly greased cookie sheet. Brush with egg white and sprinkle with nuts. Bake in preheated 350 oven for 10-12 minutes until light golden. Remove to rack to cool. Store in loosely covered container in a cool place with waxed paper between layers. Makes 36 cookies.

OLD-FASHIONED MOLASSES COOKIES

3/4 c. shortening
1 c. sugar
1/4 c. molasses
1 egg
2 c. flour
1/4 tsp. salt
2 tsp. baking soda
1 tsp. cinnamon
1 tsp. ground cloves
1 tsp. ginger

Cream shortening and sugar. Add molasses and egg. Beat well. Add dry ingredients and mix well. Roll into small balls; dip in sugar. Place on greased cookie sheet. Bake 8-10 minutes at 350. Makes 5-6 dozen cookies.

ALMOND COOKIES

1 stick margarine, softened
1 c. sugar
1 egg
1 tsp. almond extract
1 2 3/4-oz. package instant potatoes
1 1/2 c. Bisquick
Almond slices, optional

Cream margarine; add sugar gradually. Beat in egg and almond extract. Add instant potato flakes and Bisquick, beating until well mixed. Roll dough into marble-size pieces; make slight indentation in top. Bake on a greased cookie sheet at 350 about 12 minutes. A sliced almond may be pressed into each cookie before baking. Makes 6 dozen cookies.

SHAKER JELLY DOT COOKIES

1 stick Danish-type margarine
1/4 c. light brown sugar, firmly packed
1/4 tsp. salt
1 egg yolk
1/2 tsp. vanilla
1 c. sifted flour
1-3 c. filberts, pecans or walnuts, finely chopped
Jelly

In a medium mixing bowl cream margarine, sugar, salt, egg yolk and vanilla. Gradually stir in flour, blending well. Cover and chill until firm enough to handle. Work with half of dough at a time, keeping remaining portion refrigerated. Shape dough into balls about the size of marbles. Roll in nuts. Place 1" apart on ungreased cookie sheets; gently press thumb into center of each cookie to make a shallow indentations; fill indentations with jelly. Bake in preheated 350 oven until lightly browned for 10-12 minutes. With a spatula remove to wire racks to cool. Store in tightly covered tin box. Makes about 3 dozen cookies.

🌲 🌲 🌲 🌲 🌲

DOUBLE CHOCOLATE CHERRY COOKIES

1 1/2 c. butter or margarine, softened
1 3/4 c. sugar
2 eggs
1 Tbsp. vanilla
3 1/2 c. flour
3/4 c. cocoa
1/2 tsp. baking powder
1/2 tsp. baking soda
1/4 tsp. salt
2 6-oz. jars Maraschino cherries, drained and halved
1 6-oz. package chocolate chips
1 can condensed milk

Preheat oven to 350. Beat margarine and sugar until fluffy. Add eggs and vanilla. Mix well. Combine dry ingredients. Stir into margarine mixture. Dough will be stiff. Shape into 1" balls. Place 1" apart on ungreased cookie sheets. Press cherry half into center of each cookie. Bake 8-10 minutes. Cool. In heavy saucepan over medium heat, melt chips with milk; continue cooking about 3 minutes or until thick. Frost each cookie, covering cherry. Store loosely covered at room temperature. Makes 10 dozen cookies.

SUGARED ALMOND STICKS

1/2 c. blanched almonds, ground
2 Tbsp. sugar
1 c. all-purpose flour, sifted
1/3 c. sugar
1/4 tsp. salt
1/2 c. butter or margarine
1 egg yolk
1/4 tsp. almond extract
1 egg white, slightly beaten

Mix 2 Tbsp. of the almonds with 2 Tbsp. of sugar; set aside. Combine remaining almonds, the flour, sugar and salt. Cut in butter until the mixture resembles coarse crumbs. Add egg yolk and extract; mix well. Divide dough into six portions on lightly floured surface. Roll each portion into rope 12" long. Brush tops with beaten egg white, sprinkle with reserved almond-sugar mixture. Cut each strip into cookies 2" long. Place on ungreased cookie sheet. Bake at 350 for 14-15 minutes. Cool. Remove from baking sheet after 5 minutes.

SUGAR COOKIES

Cream:
1/2 c. butter or margarine
1/2 c. shortening
1 c. sugar
1 tsp. vanilla or almond flavoring

Add to creamed mixture:
1 egg

Stir in until smooth:
2 1/2 c. flour
1/2 tsp. soda
3/4 tsp. salt

Blend in and then chill:
2 Tbsp. milk

Roll out and cut into desired shapes. Sprinkle with sugar. Bake at 400 for about 12 minutes. Cool. Makes 5 1/2 dozen cookies.

BUTTER COOKIES

1 c. butter, softened
3/4 c. sugar
1 egg
1/2 tsp. vanilla
2 1/2 c. all-purpose flour
1 tsp. baking powder
1/4 tsp. salt
Food coloring, optional
Buttercream frosting (recipe follows)
Assorted candies and sprinkles

Cream butter. Gradually add sugar, beating well until light and fluffy. Add egg and vanilla; beat well. Combine flour, baking powder and salt. Add to creamed mixture, mixing well. Color dough with food coloring, if desired. Using cookie press, press dough into desired shapes onto ungreased cookie sheets. Bake at 350 for 10-12 minutes. Cool on racks. Decorate with buttercream frosting, assorted candies and sprinkles. Makes about 6 dozen cookies.

Buttercream frosting:
3 Tbsp. butter, softened
2 1/3 c. powdered sugar, sifted
Dash of salt
1 1/2 to 2 Tbsp. milk
1/2 tsp. vanilla
Food coloring, optional

Cream butter; gradually add powdered sugar, beating well. Add salt, milk and vanilla; mix well. Color if desired. Spread on cookies.

🌲 🌲 🌲 🌲 🌲

SWEDISH FINGER COOKIES

3 1/2 sticks butter
4 3/4 c. flour
7 Tbsp. sugar
1 tsp. almond extract
2 egg whites, slightly beaten
4 Tbsp. sugar
4 Tbsp. almonds, grated

Mix first four ingredients together. Roll out into long finger-sized rolls. Cut into 2 1/2-3" lengths. Brush with beaten egg whites. Mix together the 4 Tbsp. sugar and 4 Tbsp. grated almonds. Dip each piece into or sprinkle on the sugar mixture. Bake at 350 for 15-20 minutes until just pinkish brown.

HOLIDAY TARTS

1/2 c. butter
1 3-oz. package cream cheese
1 c. flour
Filling

Beat together butter and cream cheese. Stir in flour. Cover and chill 1 hour or until easy to handle. Shape dough into 1" balls. Press onto bottom and up sides of ungreased 1 3/4" muffin cups. Fill each with 1-2 tsp. filling. Bake at 325 for 25-30 minutes. Cool slightly and remove. Makes 24 tarts.

Variations of fillings:
Cream cheese:
   Beat 1 3-oz. package cream cheese.
   Add 1/3 c. sugar and 2 tsp. vanilla.
   Beat until smooth.
   Add 1 c. coconut and 1 c. chopped pecans.
   After baking, drizzle melted chocolate over top.

Pecan pie:
   Beat together 1 egg, 3/4 c. brown sugar, 1 Tbsp. melted butter and 1 tsp. vanilla.
   Stir in 1/2 c. chopped pecans.

Lemon:
   Beat 2 eggs, 1/2 c. sugar, 2 Tbsp. melted butter, 1/2 tsp. finely grated lemon peel and 1 Tbsp. lemon juice.
   Stir in 1/4 c. flaked coconut.

Pumpkin-sour cream:
   Beat 1 egg, 1/2 c. pumpkin, 1/3 c. sugar, 1/4 c. sour cream, 1 Tbsp. milk and 1/2 tsp. pumpkin pie spice.

COCOA PRETZELS

1 c. butter, softened
1/2 c. granulated sugar
1 large egg
1 tsp. almond extract
2 1/4 c. all-purpose flour
1/2 tsp. salt
1/3 c. unsweetened cocoa powder

Heat oven to 400. In large bowl with electric mixer at medium speed, beat butter, sugar, egg and almond extract until light and fluffy. At low speed, gradually beat in flour, salt and cocoa until well blended. Fit cookie press with large rosette tip. Press out into 2 1/2" pretzel shapes. Sprinkle with coarse sugar and bake 6-8 minutes. Make about 5 dozen.

SWEDISH CREAM WAFERS

Mix together thoroughly:
1 c. butter
1/3 c. whipping cream
2 c. flour, unsifted

Chill. Roll 1/8" thick and cut in 1 1/2" circles. Sprinkle with sugar and prick several times with fork. Bake on ungreased cookie sheet at 350 for 15-20 minutes. After cookies are cool, put together with filling. Makes 2 1/2 dozen.

Filling:
1 egg yolk
1/4 c. butter
3/4 c. powdered sugar
1/4 tsp. almond extract

Mix together and spread on cookie rounds and press together with plain round.

CHEESE CRACKERS

1 c. grated cheddar cheese, packed
3 oz. cream cheese
1/2 c. butter
1/4 tsp. tabasco
1 3/4 c. flour
1 Tbsp. poppy seed
2 Tbsp. sesame seed

Mix in order of ingredients. Roll into 1" logs and chill. Slice 1/4" thick and bake at 325 for 10 minutes, or until pale brown on edge. Do not overbake or get too brown as they turn bitter.

PIZZELLES

6 eggs
3 1/2 c. flour
1 1/2 c. sugar
1 c. margarine
4 tsp. baking powder
2 Tbsp. vanilla or anise

Beat eggs, adding sugar gradually. Beat until smooth. Add cooled, melted margarine and vanilla or anise. Sift flour and baking powder and add to egg mixture. Dough will be sticky enough to be dropped by spoon. Bake in pizzelle chef for 30 seconds. Serve plain or dusted with powdered sugar.

BUTTER PECAN COOKIES

1/2 c. butter, room temperature
3 Tbsp. powdered sugar
1 c. pecans, chopped
3/4 c. all-purpose flour
1 tsp. vanilla
1/4 c. powdered sugar

Preheat oven to 300. Lightly butter baking sheets. Using electric mixer, cream 1/2 c. butter and 3 Tbsp. powdered sugar. Mix in pecans, flour and vanilla. Form dough into 1" balls and place on buttered sheets. Bake until lightly browned for 20-25 minutes. Transfer to rack to cool. Roll in 1/4 c. sugar to coat. Store in airtight container.

JAM PUFFS

Beat in food processor:
    1 c. butter
    1/2 c. powdered sugar
    2 c. flour
    1 Tbsp. cornstarch
Filling:
    1 egg, slightly beaten
    1/2 c. sugar
    1 1/4 c. coconut
    Solo apricot filling

Use mini-muffin tins. Spray with Pam. Wet hands. Press about 1 tsp. dough into muffin tins. Mix egg, sugar and coconut together for filling. Put 1 tsp. Solo into dough cups. Add 1 tsp. coconut mixture. Bake for 25-30 minutes at 350. Hit pans on counter to remove—they WILL pop out!!

SANTA'S TREATS

1 c. shortening
1 c. brown sugar
1 c. white sugar
2 eggs
1 tsp. vanilla
1 1/2 c. flour
1 tsp. salt
1 tsp. baking soda
3 c. rolled oats
1/2 c. nuts
1 6-oz. package chocolate chips
1 c. raisins
1 c. peanuts

Cream shortening, sugars, eggs and vanilla. Blend with flour, salt, soda and oats. Add nuts, chips, raisins and peanuts. Shape into balls. Bake at 350 for 15 minutes.

CHOCOLATE SNOWBALLS II

1 1/4 c. butter or margarine
2/3 c. sugar
1 tsp. vanilla
2 c. all-purpose flour
1/8 tsp. salt
1/2 c. cocoa
2 c. pecans, chopped
1/2 c. powdered sugar

Cream butter and sugar until light and fluffy. Add vanilla extract. Add sifted flour, salt, cocoa and nuts. Mix thoroughly. Chill several hours. Form into balls like marbles. Place on ungreased cookie sheet. Bake 20 minutes at 350. Cool. Roll in powdered sugar. Makes 6 dozen cookies.

CHOCOLATE COVERED BON BON COOKIES

3 1/2 c. vanilla wafers
1/2 c. powdered sugar
1/3 c. Southern Comfort
2 Tbsp. cocoa
1/4 c. light corn syrup
1 c. walnuts, chopped

Roll out vanilla wafers with rolling pin until fine and smooth. Combine with remaining ingredients. Roll into balls and dip in 6 oz. chocolate chips, melted.* Put in refrigerator overnight. Serve cold.
*To melt chocolate chips in microwave, add 1 Tbsp. shortening and heat 2-3 minutes.

🌲 🌲 🌲 🌲 🌲

ICED CAPPUCCINO COOKIES

1/2 c. butter or margarine, softened
1/2 c. granulated sugar
1 large egg
1 1/2 tsp. vanilla
2 c. all-purpose flour
1 tsp. salt
1 Tbsp. instant espresso powder

In large bowl with electric mixer at medium speed, beat butter, sugar, egg and vanilla until light and fluffy. In second bowl combine flour, baking powder, salt and espresso powder. At low speed, beat flour mixture gradually into butter mixture to blend well. Refrigerate, covered, 1 1/2-2 hours until firm. Heat oven to 375. Work with 1/4 dough at a time; keep remainder of dough in refrigerator. Roll out to 1/4" thickness between two sheets of waxed paper and cut into 3" scalloped rounds. Place on lightly greased cookie sheets about 1" apart. Bake 5-7 minutes until firm to touch and edges are lightly browned. Cool on wire racks.

Frosting:
1 tsp. ground cinnamon
16-oz. container vanilla ready-to-spread frosting

Beat together and spread over cookies. Sprinkle with chopped toasted almonds.

PUFF PASTRY PALMIERS

1 1/2 c. unbleached flour
1/8 tsp. salt
1 c. unsalted butter, cold and cut up
1/2 c. sour cream
Sugar

In large bowl, combine flour and salt. With pastry blender, cut butter into flour until mixture resembles coarse crumbs. Stir in sour cream. Turn out onto smooth surface and knead 6-8 times, until mixture holds together. Shape into a ball; flatten slightly and wrap well. Refrigerate overnight.

Unwrap dough and cut into 4 equal pieces. Work with 1 piece at a time; refrigerate remaining pieces. Sprinkle 2 Tbsp. sugar on a sheet of waxed paper. Coat both sides of dough with sugar. Cover dough with more waxed paper and roll into a 12" × 5" rectangle. Remove paper and lightly mark halfway point of 12" side. Roll both 5" sides jelly-roll fashion toward center until they meet. Wrap well and freeze 30 minutes or refrigerate overnight. Repeat with remaining dough.

Line 2 cookie sheets with parchment paper. Place 1/4 c. sugar on waxed paper. Slice each roll 1/2" thick; dip each cut side into sugar. Place on cookie sheet 2 1/2" apart. Freeze until firm.

Adjust oven rack to top position. Preheat oven to 375. Bake 15 minutes until golden around edges. Turn cookies over; bake 5 minutes more. Cool on wire racks. Makes 3 dozen cookies.

EASY CHOCOLATE PEANUT BUTTER CUPS

1 package refrigerated chocolate chip cookie dough
1 package miniature peanut butter cups

In miniature baking cups place spoonful of cookie dough filling to 3/4 full. Bake according to package directions. As soon as cookie comes out of oven press a peanut butter cup in the middle of each cookie. Best when served warm.

TURTLE COOKIES

1/2 c. brown sugar, packed
1/2 c. butter or margarine, softened
2 Tbsp. water
1 tsp. vanilla
1 1/2 c. all-purpose flour
1/8 tsp. salt
Pecan halves
8 caramels, each cut into 1/4's

Mix brown sugar, margarine, water and vanilla. Stir in flour and salt until dough holds together. (If dough is dry, stir in 1-2 tsp. water.) Heat oven to 350. For each cookie, group 3-5 pecan halves on ungreased cookie sheet. Shape dough by teaspoonfuls around caramel pieces; press firmly onto center of each group of nuts. Bake 12-15 minutes until set but not brown. Cool. Dip tops of cookies into chocolate glaze.

Chocolate glaze:
    1 c. powdered sugar
    1 Tbsp. water
    1 oz. unsweetened chocolate, melted
    1 tsp. vanilla
Beat together until smooth. If necessary stir in more water.

🌲　🌲　🌲　🌲　🌲

DOUBLE CHOCOLATE TREASURES

1 12-oz. package semi-sweet chocolate pieces
1/2 c. margarine
3/4 c. sugar
2 eggs
1 tsp. vanilla
2 c. quick or old fashioned oats, uncooked
1 1/2 c. all-purpose flour
2 tsp. baking powder
1/4 tsp. salt
1/2 c. powdered sugar

Heat oven to 350. In heavy saucepan over low heat, melt 1 c. chocolate pieces. Stir until smooth; cool slightly. Beat together margarine and sugar until light and fluffy. Blend in eggs, vanilla and melted chocolate. Add combined dry ingredients except powdered sugar. Stir in remaining chocolate pieces. Shape dough into 1" balls. Roll in powdered sugar, coating heavily. Place on ungreased cookie sheet. Bake for 10-12 minutes. Cool 1 minute on cookie sheet. Remove to wire rack. Store in airtight container. Makes about 5 dozen cookies.

CHRISTMAS FRUIT BALLS

1 lb. pitted dates
1/2 c. pecans, chopped
2 4-oz. cans shredded coconut
1/2 tsp. salt
15-oz. can condensed milk
Candied cherries, cut in half

Combine dates, nuts and coconut. Add salt and milk. Blend well. Shape into 1" balls. Place on slightly greased cookie sheet. Top each ball with 1/2 cherry. Bake at 325 for 15 minutes. Remove from cookie sheet immediately.

BASIC ROLL COOKIES

Cream:
1/2 c. white or brown sugar
1/2 c. butter
Beat in:
1 tsp. vanilla
2 eggs
2 1/2 c. all-purpose flour, sifted
2 tsp. baking powder
1/2 tsp. salt

Chill dough 3-4 hours before rolling. Preheat over to 375. To roll use as little extra flour as possible. Using a roller cutter eliminates handling the dough. Bake for 7-10 minutes. May be decorated with sugar, sugar and cinnamon or colored sugar, glazes and nuts.

Chocolate glaze:
2 Tbsp. cocoa
1 Tbsp. oil
1 c. confectioners' sugar
1 Tbsp. plus 2 tsp. water
1 Tbsp. corn syrup

Combine all ingredients except sugar. Cook and stir over low heat until mixture is smooth. Remove from heat. Beat in sugar. Spread over cookies.

COCONUT BELLS

1/4 tsp. salt
3/4 c. butter or margarine
2/3 c. granulated sugar
1 3/4 c. flour
1 egg
1/4 tsp. coconut flavoring or anise flavoring
Red and green candy-coated milk chocolates

In large mixer bowl, beat margarine and salt with mixer on medium speed for 30 seconds. Add sugar and beat until fluffly. Add egg and extract; beat well. Add flour and beat until mixed. Cover and chill about 30 minutes or until easy to handle.

Divide dough in half. Shape dough into two 6" rolls. Roll each half in colored sugar. Wrap in moisture proof wrap. Freeze dough 4-6 hours until firm. May be kept frozen up to 6 months.

To bake: let stand at room temperature for 5 minutes. Cut into 1/4" thick slices. Let stand 10 minutes to soften. Place on ungreased cookie sheets. Fold sides of slice to overlapping and place chocolate piece on the bottom of the bell. Bake at 350 for 10-12 minutes or until edges are lightly brown. Makes about 4 dozen cookies.

BIG FELLOW SUGAR COOKIES

Sift together and set aside:
2 c. sifted flour (may have to add a little more)
1 1/2 tsp. baking powder
1/2 tsp. salt

Cream:
1/2 c. butter or margarine
1 tsp. vanilla

Add gradually:
3/4 c. sugar

Beat mixture until fluffy then add:
2 eggs, well beaten

Gradually stir in dry ingredients and blend well. Chill thoroughly in refrigerator. Roll cookie dough 1/8" thick; cut with cookie cutter. Sprinkle tops of cookies with sugar. Place on cookie sheet. Bake at 375 for 10-12 minutes. Remove immediately to rack to cool. Makes 1 1/2 dozen cookies. (A 1 lb. coffee tin with rim removed makes an ideal cutter.)

ALMOND BUTTER STICKS

3/4 c. sugar
2 tsp. almond flavoring
1/3 c. plus 1 Tbsp. butter, softened
2 3-oz. package cream cheese
2 c. mix (make-ahead mix recipe follows)
1 egg, separated (reserve white for glazing)
1/4 c. almonds, sliced

Make-ahead mix:
1 1/2 c. butter or margarine, softened
1 Tbsp. salt
2 tsp. baking powder
6 c. all-purpose flour

In a very large bowl, combine butter, salt and baking powder; using electric mixer, blend well. Lightly spoon flour into measuring cup; level off (do not scoop or sift flour). Add flour to butter mixture; blend until fine crumbs form. Store tightly covered in refrigerator up to 4 weeks. Makes 8 cups mix.

Preheat oven to 375. Grease cookie sheet. In small bowl, stir together sugar and almond flavoring; cover and set aside. In medium bowl, combine 1/3 c. butter, cream cheese and egg yolk; blend until smooth. (Dip measuring cup into cookie mix; level off). Stir in mix. Knead on floured surface about 14 strokes until pliable. Roll or press out to a 12" x 12" square. Spread with 1 Tbsp. butter. Cut dough in half; place one half on greased cookie sheet. Spoon sugar mixture to within 1/2" of dough edges. Place remaining dough half, buttered side down, over sugar. Press edges tightly to seal. Brush with slightly beaten egg white; sprinkle with almonds. Bake 20-30 minutes until golden brown. Cool at least 20 minutes. Remove from cookie sheet. Cut pastry in half lengthwise and in 1/2" strips crosswise. Makes 48 cookies.

GINGERBREAD SPRITZ

1 c. butter or margarine, softened
1/2 c. molasses
1/4 c. brown sugar, packed
1 egg
1 tsp. vanilla
2 3/4 c. all-purpose flour
1/2 tsp. baking powder

1/2 tsp. ground nutmeg
1/2 tsp. ground cinnamon
1/4 tsp. salt
1/4 tsp. ground cloves
1/4 tsp. ground ginger
1 recipe powdered sugar glaze,
  optional

In mixer bowl, beat together the butter, molasses and brown sugar. Add egg and vanilla. Beat well. In another bowl thoroughly stir together flour, baking powder, nutmeg, cinnamon, salt, cloves and ginger. Add to creamed mixture. Stir until thoroughly mixed. Cover and chill dough 1-2 hours.

Fill cookie press with half the dough. Press into desired shapes onto an ungreased cookie sheet. Repeat with remaining dough. Bake at 400 for 7-8 minutes or until set. Remove from cookie sheets; cool on wire rack. If desired, drizzle cookies with powder sugar glaze. Makes 4 dozen cookies.

Powdered sugar glaze:
    1 c. sifted powdered sugar
    1/4 tsp. vanilla
    About 1 Tbsp. milk
Stir together. Should be of drizzling consistency.

♠ ♠ ♠ ♠ ♠

DATE ROLL COOKIES

2 1/4 c. dates, chopped
1 c. white sugar
1 c. water
1 c. nuts, chopped
1/3 tsp. salt

1/2 tsp. soda
1 c. shortening
2 c. brown sugar
3 eggs, well beaten
4 c. flour

Cook dates, sugar and water slowly for 10 minutes. Add nuts and cool. Cream shortening and brown sugar. Add eggs. Beat thoroughly. Beat in flour and soda. Roll out dough and spread with date filling. Roll and refrigerate overnight. Cut into 1/8" slices. Bake at 400 for 10-12 minutes. Makes 5 dozen.

HOLIDAY DATE-NUT BARS

1 8-oz. package pitted dates, chopped
1 c. raisins, chopped
1 c. walnuts, chopped
1 tsp. grated orange peel
1 1/2 tsp. cinnamon
1 c. sugar
1/4 lb. butter or margarine, room temperature
1 tsp. vanilla
2 eggs
2 c. all-purpose flour
2 tsp. baking powder
1/2 tsp. salt
2 Tbsp. orange juice
Powdered sugar

Preheat oven to 375. Grease 2 baking sheets; set aside. In large bowl, stir dates, raisins, walnuts, orange peel, cinnamon and 1/2 c. sugar until fruit is coated with sugar; set aside. In a separate bowl, cream butter, the remaining 1/2 c. sugar and vanilla until fluffy. Beat in eggs, 1 at a time, mixing well after each addition. Stir in flour, baking powder, salt and orange juice. Add date mixture. Stir until blended. Do not over mix. Dough will be very stiff. Divide dough into 4 portions. Shape 2 logs on each prepared baking sheet. Make logs about 12" x 2" x 1/2". Bake 15 minutes. Although they will be slightly brown, logs will feel very soft and underdone. They will become firm as they cool. Cool 15 minutes. Cut diagonally into 3/4" bars. Dust with powdered sugar. May be frozen. Makes 64 bars.

APRICOT RUGELACH

2 c. all-purpose flour
butter or margarine
3/4 c. sour cream
6 Tbsp. apricot preserves
6 Tbsp. semi-sweet chocolate pieces
1/3 c. almonds, sliced
2 Tbsp. sugar

1. Measure flour into large bowl. With pastry blender, cut in 1 c. butter until mixture resembles small peas. With spoon, stir in sour cream just until dough holds together. Divide dough into three pieces. Wrap each piece in plastic wrap. Refrigerate 1 hour or until firm enough to handle.

2. On lightly floured surface, with floured rolling pin, roll 1 piece of chilled dough into an 11" round, keeping remaining dough refrigerated. Spread dough with 2 Tbsp. apricot preserves. Sprinkle with 2 Tbsp. chocolate pieces. Cut dough round into 12 equal wedges. Starting at curved edge, roll up each wedge, jelly roll fashion. Place cookies, point-side down, about 1 1/2" apart, on large cookie sheet. Repeat with remaining dough, preserves and chocolate pieces.

3. Preheat oven to 375. In small saucepan over low heat, melt 2 Tbsp. butter. In small bowl, mix almonds and sugar. Brush cookies with melted butter. Sprinkle with almond mixture.

4. Bake cookies 25 minutes or until golden brown. Immediately remove cookies to wire racks to cool. Store cookies in tightly covered container. Makes 3 dozen cookies.

POWDERED SUGAR COOKIES

Stir by hand—don't use a mixer.

1 c. butter or margarine
1 egg, beaten
1 tsp. vanilla
1 c. powdered sugar
2 c. flour
pinch of salt
1/2 tsp. soda
1/2 tsp. cream of tartar

Sift dry ingredients together. Cut in butter as in pie crust. Add beaten egg and vanilla. Mix all together. Roll in balls. Flatten with a glass dipped in sugar. Bake at 400 for 8-10 minutes.

ALMOND CRESCENT COOKIES

1 c. butter
1/2 c. powdered sugar
2/3 c. ground almonds
2 c. flour
1/2 tsp. vanilla
1/2 tsp. almond extract

Cream butter and sifted sugar. Add almonds. Add flour and extract alternately. Bake at 350 for 10 minutes. Sprinkle top with powdered sugar.

SNOW CAP COOKIES

2 c. semi-sweet chocolate chips
3/4 c. butter or margarine, softened
3/4 c. confectioners' sugar
2 eggs, separated
1 1/2 tsp. vanilla
1 1/2 c. quick or old fashioned oats, uncooked
1 c. flour
1/4 tsp. salt, optional
1/8 tsp. cream of tartar
1/2 c. granulated sugar

In small saucepan over low heat, melt 1 1/2 c. chocolate chips; cool slightly. In large bowl, beat together butter and confectioners' sugar until light and fluffy. Blend in chocolate, egg yolks and 1 tsp. vanilla. Stir in oats, flour and salt. Mix well. Shape into 1/2" balls. (Do not let dough stand more than 30 minutes before forming balls.) Place on ungreased cookie sheet. Press cookies into 1 1/2" flat circles with palm of hand or base of glass. Preheat oven to 325. Combine egg whites, remaining 1/2 tsp. vanilla and cream of tartar. Beat at high speed of mixer until soft peaks form. Gradually add sugar, beating until stiff, glossy peaks form. Fold in remaining 1/2 c. chocolate chips. Top each cookie with 1 tsp. meringue. Bake 12-15 minutes or until meringue becomes firm and light golden brown. Immediately remove to wire racks to cool. Store loosely covered. Makes 6 dozen cookies.

LEMON-PISTACHIO DROPS

1 c. butter or margarine, room temperature
1 c. granulated sugar
2 large eggs, separated
2 tsp. lemon peel, freshly grated
3 Tbsp. lemon juice, fresh
2 1/3 c. all-purpose flour
3/4 c. pistachio nuts or pecans, chopped finely
52 shelled whole pistachio nuts or small pecan halves

Heat oven to 350. Lightly grease cookie sheets. Beat butter and sugar in large bowl with electric mixer until fluffy. Beat in egg yolks, lemon peel and lemon juice until blended. Gradually beat in flour just until well blended. If necessary, refrigerate dough until firm enough to handle. In a shallow bowl, beat egg whites with a fork until foamy. Place chopped nuts on waxed paper. Shape rounded teaspoonfuls of dough into 52 1" balls. Dip in egg white, then roll in nuts to coat. Place 1" apart on prepared cookie sheets. Press a nut into top of each ball. Bake 15-18 minutes until firm and set. Remove to wire rack to cool. Makes 52 cookies.

🌲 🌲 🌲 🌲 🌲

COCOA MINT WAFERS

1 1/2 c. all-purpose flour
3/4 c. unsweetened cocoa powder, preferably Dutch process
1 1/4 tsp. baking powder
1/8 tsp. salt
3/4 c. butter or margarine, at room temperature
1 1/4 c. granulated sugar
1 large egg
24 rectangular mint parfait wafers
    melted with 1 Tbsp. shortening

Mix flour, cocoa, baking powder and salt. Beat butter and sugar in large bowl with electric mixer until light and fluffy. Beat in egg. Gradually stir in flour mixture until blended. Divide dough in half. Shape each half into a roll 1 1/2" in diameter. Wrap and freeze or chill about 4 hours until very firm. Heat oven to 375. Lightly grease cookie sheets. Cut rolls in 1/4" thick slices. Place 1" apart on prepared cookie sheets. Bake for 10-12 minutes until cookies look dry. Remove to a rack to cool completely. Cookies are soft when hot but crisp when cool. Drizzle mint mixture over tops. Refrigerate 15 minutes for chocolate to harden. Makes 64.

CHINESE CHEWS

An excellent keeper in tins.

3/4-1 c. sugar
2 eggs, beaten
1 c. nuts, chopped
1/2 tsp. baking powder
1/4 tsp. salt
8 oz. dates, chopped
1/2 -1 tsp. cinnamon
Powdered sugar

Beat eggs until foamy; gradually beat in sugar. Beat until quite thick. Add all remaining ingredients and mix well. Spread into lightly greased or "Pammed" 9" square pan.

Bake at 350 for 20 minutes or until top is golden brown. Center of dough will feel sticky and not fully baked. While warm, roll into balls. Roll in powdered sugar and cool on rack.

🌲 🌲 🌲 🌲 🌲

CINNAMON LOGS/CREAM CHEESE ROLL-UPS

1- 1 1/2 loaves white bread with crusts removed
    and rolled as flat as you can.
2 8-oz. packages cream cheese, softened
2 egg yolks
1/2 c. sugar

Combine cream cheese, egg yolks and sugar. Spread mixture on bread and roll into logs. Dip in 1 1/2 c. melted butter. Roll in a mixture of 1 Tbsp. cinnamon and 1 c. sugar.

Variation 1: Freeze on cookie sheets. Bake before serving at 400 for 10-15 minutes.

Variation 2: Bake at 350 seam side down for about 15 minutes or until brown. These will freeze very well. If they get soggy, just bake in the oven for a short time.

CHEERY CHERRY CHEWIES

1 c. all-purpose flour, unsifted
1/2 c. powdered sugar
1 c. butter or margarine, softened
1 large egg
2 tsp. vanilla
2 c. red and green cherries, coarsely chopped
1 c. walnuts or pecans, coarsely chopped

Preheat oven to 375. Grease 2 baking sheets. In large bowl, beat first 5 ingredients. Mix in cherries and nuts. Shape 2 11" rolls. Wrap in plastic wrap. Freeze 1 hour or until firm. Cut into 1/4" slices. Place on sheets 1 1/2" apart. Bake 12 minutes until golden brown. Remove from sheets and cool. Makes 6 dozen cookies.

ALMOND CHRISTMAS WREATH COOKIES

1 1/2 c. water
3/4 c. butter
1 1/2 c. flour
5 eggs
2 tsp. almond extract
1 c. almond, finely chopped

Preheat oven to 400. Heat water and butter to rolling boil. Reduce heat. Stir in flour until mixture forms ball (about 1 minute). Remove from heat. Beat in eggs and almond extract. Drop by teaspoonfuls 1" apart on ungreased baking sheets. Shape into wreath using teaspoon handle to make center hole. Bake for 20-25 minutes until puffed and golden. Cool. Dip in frosting then in almonds. Makes 6 dozen cookies.

Almond Frosting:
1 1/2 c. powdered sugar
2 Tbsp. butter
2 Tbsp. water
1/2 tsp. almond extract
Green food coloring

Mix together until smooth.

INDEX

Name _____

Address _____

City/State/Zip _____ Telephone (_____) _____

Please send best-selling Colorado Collection cookbooks as indicated below:

	QUANTITY	PRICE	TAX (Colorado residents only)	TOTAL
COLORADO COOKIE COLLECTION	_____	$12.95	$ .39 per book	$ _____
NOTHIN' BUT MUFFINS	_____	$ 9.95	$ .30 per book	$ _____
	_____		Plus $2.00 each for shipping and handling	$ _____
			TOTAL ENCLOSED	$ _____

SEND A GIFT TO SOMEONE SPECIAL

Name _____

Address_____

City/State/Zip _____

Message _____

_____

Please make checks payable to:

C & G Publishing, Inc.
2702 19th St. Rd.
Greeley, CO 80631
1-800-925-3172

. . . .

Name _____

Address _____

City/State/Zip _____ Telephone (_____) _____

Please send best-selling Colorado Collection cookbooks as indicated below:

	QUANTITY	PRICE	TAX (Colorado residents only)	TOTAL
COLORADO COOKIE COLLECTION	_____	$12.95	$ .39 per book	$ _____
NOTHIN' BUT MUFFINS	_____	$ 9.95	$ .30 per book	$ _____
	_____		Plus $2.00 each for shipping and handling	$ _____
			TOTAL ENCLOSED	$ _____

SEND A GIFT TO SOMEONE SPECIAL

Name _____

Address_____

City/State/Zip _____

Message _____

_____

Please make checks payable to:

C & G Publishing, Inc.
2702 19th St. Rd.
Greeley, CO 80631
1-800-925-3172